YOUR KNOWLEDGE HA

- We will publish your bachelor's and master's thesis, essays and papers

- Your own eBook and book -
  sold worldwide in all relevant shops

- Earn money with each sale

Upload your text at www.GRIN.com
and publish for free

Bibliographic information published by the German National Library:

The German National Library lists this publication in the National Bibliography; detailed bibliographic data are available on the Internet at http://dnb.dnb.de .

This book is copyright material and must not be copied, reproduced, transferred, distributed, leased, licensed or publicly performed or used in any way except as specifically permitted in writing by the publishers, as allowed under the terms and conditions under which it was purchased or as strictly permitted by applicable copyright law. Any unauthorized distribution or use of this text may be a direct infringement of the author s and publisher s rights and those responsible may be liable in law accordingly.

Imprint:

Copyright © 2018 GRIN Verlag
Print and binding: Books on Demand GmbH, Norderstedt Germany
ISBN: 9783668997080

This book at GRIN:

https://www.grin.com/document/494016

Abdulkarim Ajouaou Saidi

Valuation of Crypto Assets. A Conceptual Framework and Case Application to the IOTA Token

GRIN Verlag

GRIN - Your knowledge has value

Since its foundation in 1998, GRIN has specialized in publishing academic texts by students, college teachers and other academics as e-book and printed book. The website www.grin.com is an ideal platform for presenting term papers, final papers, scientific essays, dissertations and specialist books.

Visit us on the internet:

http://www.grin.com/

http://www.facebook.com/grincom

http://www.twitter.com/grin_com

Berlin School of Economics and Law

Accounting and Controlling (Master of Arts)

Master Thesis

VALUATION OF CRYPTO ASSETS - A CONCEPTUAL FRAMEWORK AND CASE APPLICATION TO THE IOTA TOKEN

written by

Abdulkarim Ajouaou Saidi

Berlin, July 30th 2018

Table of contents

List of abbreviations IV

List of figures VI

List of tables VII

1. Introduction 1

2. Objective and approach of the thesis 2

3. Terminology and definitions 4

    3.1   Definition of distributed ledger technology and blockchain 4

    3.2   Definition and classification of crypto assets 6

    3.3   About the fundamental value of crypto assets 10

4. Conceptual framework: Valuation techniques of crypto assets 12

    4.1   Discounted Cash Flow (DCF) and CAPM 14

    4.2   Asset rotation theory 16

    4.3   Equation of Exchange (Quantity Theory of Money) 18

    4.4   Network Value to Transaction (NVT) ratio 24

    4.5   Metcalfe's Law 29

    4.6   Cost of production approach 31

    4.7   Accessibility discount 34

    4.8   Key findings 36

5. Case application: Valuation of the IOTA token 37

5.1	About IOTA	37
5.2	Valuation of IOTA	40
6.	Conclusion	49
List of references		51
Appendices		57

List of abbreviations

Bn	Billion
BRA	Blockchain Research Accelerator
BTC	Bitcoin
CAGR	Compound Annual Growth Rate
Cap	Capitalization
CAPM	Capital Asset Pricing Model
CFTC	Commodity Futures Trading Commission
Co	Company
CUV	Current utility value
E.g	Exempli gratia
EUR	Euro
DAA	Daily active address
DAG	Directed Acyclic Graph
DCF	Discounted cash flow
DEUV	Discounted expected utility value
DLT	Distributed ledger technology
ERC	Ethereum Request for Comment
ETF	Exchange-traded fund
EU	European Union
FOMO	Fear of missing out
FX	Foreign exchange
GB	Gigabyte

GDP	Gross domestic product
ICO	Initial coin offering
ID	Identity
IFRS	International Financial Reporting Standards
IIoT	Industrial Internet of Things
IoT	Internet of Things
LSE	London Stock Exchange
M2M	Machine-to-machine
MAU	Monthly active users
MIOTA	Million IOTA
MOBI	Mobility Open Blockchain Initiative
NVT	Network Value to Transaction
NASDAQ	National Association of Securities Dealers Automated Quotations
NYSE	New York Stock Exchange
P2P	Peer-to-Peer
P/E	Price-to-earnings ratio
PoC	Proof of Concept
RWTH	Rheinisch-Westfälische Technische Hochschule
SEC	Securities and Exchange Commission
S&P	Standard & Poor's
TAM	Total addressable market
USA	United States of America
USD	United States dollar

List of figures

Figure 1: Total market cap of all crypto assets in 2017/18 1

Figure 2: Illustration of centralized ledger and distributed ledger 5

Figure 3: Bitcoin network value and NVT ratio from 2012 to 2017 25

Figure 4: Bitcoin network value and refined NVT ratio – overvaluation 27

Figure 5: Bitcoin network value and refined NVT ratio – undervaluation 27

Figure 6: Upper and lower bound for Bitcoin value 30

Figure 7: Actual and estimated Bitcoin value 30

Figure 8: Ratio of Bitcoin market price to model price 33

Figure 9: Monero price appreciation after Bithumb listing 34

Figure 10: Development of DLT protocols from 2012 to 2017 37

Figure 11: Illustration of blockchain vs. IOTA Tangle 38

Figure 12: Transaction confirmation in the IOTA Tangle 38

Figure 13: Percent penetration of IOTA from 2019 to 2028 45

List of tables

Table 1: Bitcoin target markets and required monetary base in 2025 20

Table 2: PQV growth ratio (r_{PQ}/r_V) 23

Table 3: Key findings – conceptual part 36

Table 4: IOTA target markets in 2028 44

1. Introduction

2017 was a landmark year for crypto assets, such as Bitcoin or Ethereum. The total market cap rocketed from around $15 billion in January 2017 to over $700 billion in January 2018 (see **Figure 1**). The leading cryptocurrency Bitcoin hit its all-time high of almost $20,000 per coin on December 17th, 2017 finishing the year worth more than 1,300% of its value of around $1,000 at the beginning of the year (CoinMarketCap, 2018). Millions of people entered the new market around the world. The extremely high increase was characterized by low correlation with other financial assets. Even though crypto assets are still in an early and immature stage of their existence, many leading investors and thinkers in the crypto space consider them as a new asset class.

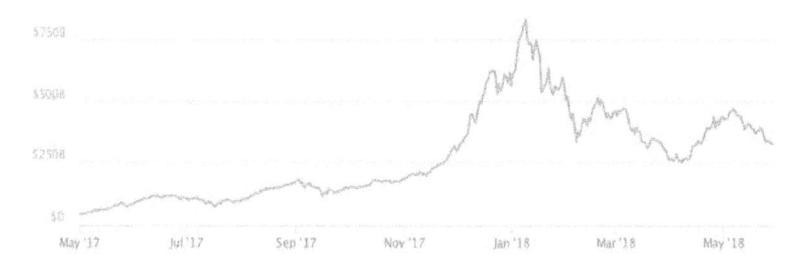

Figure 1: Total market cap of all crypto assets in 2017/18 (CoinMarketCap, 2018)

The above chart (**Figure 1**) illustrates that Bitcoin and co are very volatile compared to other asset classes. In the world of crypto assets, it is not unusual that a token's market price raises or drops by more than 100% within a few days. Obviously, these extreme price fluctuations do not necessarily reflect the underlying value of a crypto asset. The price is rather driven by hype and even market manipulation. This leads to the question: If the price does not represent the value, what is the fundamental value of a crypto asset? And how could this value be calculated? In the traditional financial world, fundamental analysis based on financial statements is used to evaluate stocks of a company. Since there are no financial statements for crypto assets new valuation techniques need to be developed, that comply with the different features of this emerging asset class.

2. Objective and approach of the thesis

This thesis aims at elaborating fundamental valuation techniques for crypto assets. Since research in this field is still at the very beginning this work intends to provide investors, financial analysts, token issuers, researchers or crypto enthusiasts a framework of how to determine the fundamental value of this emerging asset class. To do so, three main research questions are formulated:

1. How can the fundamental value of crypto assets be determined?
2. Which valuation techniques can be applied to the different token types?
3. What is the fundamental value of the IOTA token?

In order to answer the questions, the thesis will progress in the following manner: First, the reader will be introduced to distributed ledger technology (DLT) and blockchain, which represent the underlying technology of crypto assets. In the next step the term 'crypto asset' will be defined. It will be elaborated to what extent crypto assets can be considered as a new asset class and how crypto assets can be classified into different types. The terminological part will end up with a discussion of the fundamental value of this new asset class.

The main body of the thesis consists of two parts, a theoretical (conceptual) and a practical (applicational) part. The theoretical part aims to collect and evaluate all current valuation methods for crypto assets. Different absolute as well as relative valuation techniques will be elaborated, namely the Discounted Cash Flow (DCF) model and CAPM, the asset rotation theory, the Equation of Exchange, the NVT ratio, Metcalfe's Law, the cost of production approach as well as the accessibility discount. At some points the current models will also be further developed. This part also discusses limitations of each model and elaborates the applicability of each model to the different token types. The conceptual framework is based on a profound literature review. Since research in this field is still at the very beginning most content is spread among very few books (Chris Burniske's piece *Cryptoassets* to be highlighted) and mainly online sources, such as reports, studies, articles or blog entries. The discussion of the models is also inspired by experts from the crypto space, especially from members of the Blockchain Research Accelerator (BRA) who assisted this master thesis.

The second part of the main body comprises a case application of one valuation model, namely the Equation of Exchange, to the IOTA token. First, the general purpose, the underlying technology, the history as well as the token design of IOTA will be presented. In the second step the fundamental value will be calculated based on an in-depth Excel analysis which can be found in the appendices (**Appendix 1**). The input parameters are based on forecasts of market research firms, expert opinions from members of the BRA and personal assumptions. Three different scenarios of market penetration of the IOTA token will be conducted which results in a lower and upper bound of a present fundamental value of the IOTA token. The conceptual part ends up with a discussion of the results and limitations as well as the risks related to the IOTA project.

The conclusion will be summing up the key findings of this thesis by referring to the above research questions. It also comprises a discussion of the limitations as well as a future outlook of the research topic.

3. Terminology and definitions

The rise of the crypto ecosystem created a lot of new terminologies that are very often not clearly defined in literature. Nearly everyone has already heard of terms such as blockchain or Bitcoin, but only a few people are able to explain them and their underlying technology in a simple and comprehensible way. Casually spoken, the famous American talk show host John Oliver described crypto assets as "everything you don't understand about money combined with everything you don't understand about computers" (Oliver, 2018). This section explains briefly the basic terms that are relevant for this thesis and the general understanding of the topic. By reading it the reader should be able to grasp the meaning of terms such as distributed ledger technology, blockchain, crypto assets and the fundamental value.

3.1 Definition of distributed ledger technology and blockchain

It is quite important to understand how the underlying technology of crypto assets, namely distributed ledger technology and blockchain, work in order to understand how crypto assets derive their value.

The World Bank defines distributed ledger technology, short DLT, as a new and fast-evolving approach to record and share data across multiple ledgers, which each have the exact same data records. You can think of DLT as just a distributed database that eliminates the control over the ledgers by one central entity (World Bank, 2017, p. 1). The decentralized nature of DLT allows all participants in a peer-to-peer network to record any kind of "reality" such as ownership, transaction records, knowledge etc. without relying on a trusted central party. There exists, at any point in time, only one version of the ledger and each network participant owns a full and up-to-date copy of the entire ledger (World Bank, 2017, p. 5). The following graph (**Figure 2**) illustrates the general functioning of DLT compared to centralized ledgers:

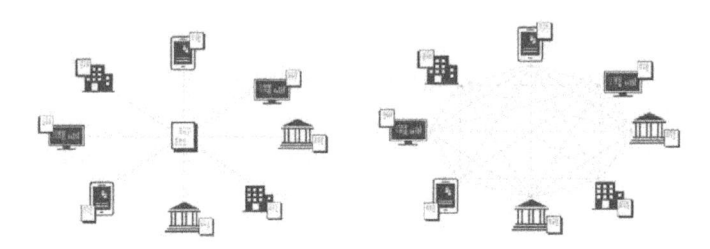

Figure 2: Illustration of centralized ledger (left) and distributed ledger (right) (Source: World Bank, 2017, p.7)

In the centralized ledger all parties reconcile their local databases with a centralized electronic ledger that is maintained and controlled by a trusted central party e.g. a bank (World Bank, 2017, p. 7). In the distributed ledger each node in a P2P network owns a full and up-to-date copy of the entire ledger. Every proposed local addition to the ledger by a network participant is communicated across the network to all nodes. Nodes collectively validate the addition through a cryptographic consensus mechanism. After validation is confirmed, the new addition is added to all ledgers to ensure data consistency across the entire network (World Bank, 2017, p. 7).

DLT shows significant advantages over centralized ledger systems. As already mentioned it removes the need for an intermediary or central authority. This can translate into lower costs, better scalability and faster time to market. Since all members have a full copy of the distributed ledger, DLT also provide greater transparency, immutability and easier auditability than traditional systems. DLT also provide the possibility of programming "smart contracts". These digital contracts are automatically executed once certain conditions are satisfied, for example invoices that are paid automatically once a shipment arrives. Furthermore, DLT is considered as more resilient against cyber-attacks because of its distributed nature (World Bank, 2017, p. 15 f.).

It should also be emphasized that DLT is not one single, well-defined technology. Instead, every DLT that exists differs in its design and functionality depending on its purpose. Blockchain is the first and by far the most common type of DLT. It stores and transmits data in packages called "blocks" that are connected to each other in a digital 'chain' (World Bank, 2017).

The first application of DLT, more specifically blockchain, was the cryptocurrency Bitcoin. In 2008, the white paper "Bitcoin: A Peer-to-Peer Electronic Cash System" was published by an unidentified person or group of persons using the pseudonym Satoshi Nakamoto. The Bitcoin blockchain was designed with the specific intention of creating a digital currency that is free from central control and anonymizes the identities of its network participant (World Bank, 2017, p. 4). Due to limitations of the Bitcoin protocol, such as limited scalability and high transaction fees, a bunch of other DLT networks such as Ethereum, Ripple or IOTA were developed in the last years.

Even though DLT has been closely linked to digital currencies, various other DLT and blockchain applications exist or are under development. There is a particularly strong interest in DLT in the financial sector: at the time of publication, at least half of the top 30 banks are engaging in blockchain proofs of concepts. Stock exchanges around the world are also investigating and testing DLT to improve securities trading platforms, including NASDAQ, NYSE, and LSE. DLT could disrupt the way stocks are issued and traded, and in the long term potentially replace existing trading platforms. Other typical sectors that are exploring DLT solutions are trade and commerce, agriculture, governance, healthcare and humanitarian aid (World Bank, 2017, p. 21 f.).

3.2 Definition and classification of crypto assets

After looking at the underlying technology, it is necessary to clearly define the term 'crypto-asset'. The fundamental questions that need to be answered here are: How can crypto assets be defined? Can they be considered as assets? If so, do they fall under traditional asset classes or do they represent an entirely new asset class? And finally, what are the different types of crypto assets?

Crypto assets are digital assets recorded on a distributed ledger (usually blockchain). They derive their name from the cryptographic security mechanisms used within distributed ledgers. Cryptography is used to verify transactions and secure the network without the intervention of a central party (EY, 2018). In fact, the term crypto asset refers to any kind of token that is created based on DLT through an ICO ("Initial Coin Offering") (D'Onorio Demeo & Young, 2017, p. 4). Therefore, the terms crypto asset and token are used as interchangeable synonyms in this work. Some authors also distinguish between tokens and coins, stating that a coin is built in its own blockchain protocol (e.g. Bitcoin or Ethereum) and a token is implemented on top of another blockchain protocol, for example all ERC-20 tokens are implemented on the Ethereum blockchain (Koenig, 2017, p. 50). However, for the purpose of this thesis this distinction is not necessary, and both terms are used as equivalents of the term crypto asset.

Generally speaking, an asset is defined as something that has a monetary value (costs, book value, market value or residual value), and that an entity purchases, owns, benefits from or has use of, in generating income. An asset can be physical (cash, machinery, inventory, land and building…) or non-physical (patents, account receivables, stocks, bonds, goodwill…). Furthermore, assets are characterized by being convertible into cash (BusinessDictionary, n.d.). Since crypto assets clearly fulfil all these definition criteria, they can be considered as assets.

The question whether crypto assets represent a new asset class is not that simple. According to Wikipedia an asset class is defined as a group of assets "which have similar financial characteristics, behave similarly in the marketplace […] and are often subject to the same laws and regulations" (Wikipedia, n.d.). As already outlined, crypto assets have very different financial characteristics compared to other asset classes such as stocks or bonds. They don't necessarily pay out any dividends or interest rates. They are based on DLT which is not the case for traditional asset classes. Usually an investor in crypto assets receives tokens that can be sent, received, and earned through the participation in the DLT or blockchain. The price of a token depends on the supply and demand on so called crypto exchanges such as Coinbase, Binance or Bitfinex. Currently around 1600 different tokens exist with a total market cap of about $300 billion at the time of writing (CoinMarketCap, 2018). In 2017, the combined market cap rocketed from $15 billion in January to over $600 billion at year-end. This outstanding raise was accompanied by low correlations to other asset classes. The spectrum of crypto investors is quite broad, ranging from tech-savvy teenagers, high-net worth professionals to even highly sophisticated hedge fonds and institutions. Especially more and more institutional investments are expected to enter the crypto space (Horsley,

2017). Due to this development billionaire investor Mike Novogratz believes that "crypto markets will reach $20 trillion value" (Njui, 2018). All these specifications are tempting to consider crypto assets as a completely new asset class. However, from a legal and regulatory perspective they are not treated in a uniform way. While some nations such as China strictly prohibited the trading of crypto assets, others are welcoming them as a legitimate investment. Many regulators try to put them into legal classifications of existing laws. In the USA for example, it currently depends on the nature of a token weather it is legally treated as a security, commodity or anything else. In that framework, tokens that are developed by a single, centralized entity such as a corporation might be considered as securities. These tokens have to meet all the SEC requirements for securities. Other tokens, that are for example, backed by an underlying commodity, might be considered as a commodity under the supervision U.S. Commodity Futures Trading Commission (CFTC) (Fung, 2018). Tokens that do not fall under these definitions are considered as utility tokens and stay unaffected by regulation. All in all, it can be said that the regulators do not per se consider crypto assets as an entirely new asset class, but rather categorize them within existing frameworks according to their nature. However, this is does not lead to the conclusion that crypto assets cannot be seen as a distinct asset class. Regulatory steps towards crypto assets are still at the beginning and the future will show how they will be treated by the law makers. It can be assumed that a well-balanced regulation of the crypto market will strengthen the legitimacy of crypto assets as a new asset class since more people will feel more comfortable to invest their money in crypto assets. For now, they could be described as a new asset class in the nascent stage.

As the law makers noticed correctly, there are various types of crypto assets, also referred to as tokens, which will be explained in the following. Generally, tokens can be broken down into four types: Utility tokens, security tokens, cryptocurrencies and asset backed tokens (Hahn & Wons, 2018, p. 10).

A utility token is characterized by a specific functionality ("utility") within a DLT network or platform. Utility tokens provide the user (future) access to a good or service, which in most cases, have yet to be developed. A utility token might be best compared to a gift card or software license, for example. The vast majority of ICOs that launched in 2016 and 2017 generated utility tokens (Hahn & Wons, 2018, p. 10). Ethereum is the best-known example of a utility token. Ethereum provides the platform to create smart contracts (code that can execute transactions automatically). Furthermore, other tokens (so called "ERC-20 tokens") as well as decentralized apps ("dapps") can be built on top of the Ethereum network. Augur, for instance, is a decentralized prediction market built on top of Ethereum where users can place bets on outcomes, like which team will win the World Cup, and be compensated for being right.

A security token (also equity token) has similar characteristics to traditional securities such as equities (stocks). It can be described as a mean of investment in a company, often associated with profit participation or other rights (Hahn & Wons, 2018, p. 10). Not so many security tokens have been issued so far, but many experts in the crypto space expect an increasing popularity of security tokens (especially equity tokens) in the near future.

Cryptocurrencies are probably the best-known token class due to the popularity of Bitcoin, "the mother of all cryptocurrencies". A cryptocurrency is a cryptography-secured digital or virtual currency operating on DLT without the control of a central bank (Hahn & Wons, 2018, p. 10). Like traditional fiat currencies (USD, EUR, etc.), cryptocurrencies primarily serve the the three main purposes of a currency being a medium of exchange, store of value and unity of account (Hosp, 2017, p. 25). Bitcoin represents the first widely-adopted and most popular cryptocurrency. Besides Bitcoin, over 1000 different "altcoins" (stands for alternative cryptocurrency coins) have been introduced over the past few years and many central banks are actively exploring the possibility of issuing their own cryptocurrencies. Many altcoins such as Litecoin and Bitcoin Cash are variants (forks) of Bitcoin, with modifications to the original open-sourced protocol to enable new features. Other cryptocurrencies such as Ripple created their own blockchain (Cong, et al., 2018, p. 6).

Finally, there are asset backed tokens (also referred to as crypto commodities) that represent a claim to an underlying asset (e.g. gold or other commodities, real estate…). It enables micro shares of assets (such as 0.01 wind turbines) (Hahn & Wons, 2018, p.

12). Tether, for example, is an asset backed token since every Tether is backed by 1 US Dollar. Tether is also an example for a so-called "stable coin" since it stays (almost) stable in value.

Note that tokens don't necessarily fit into one token class but can also represent so-called hybrid tokens that have features of two or more token classes. IOTA, for example can be seen as a cryptocurrency designed for micro M2M payments ("medium of exchange") but also as a utility token since it provides access to the IOTA network ('the Tangle'). The IOTA network can be used among others for secured data transmission.

3.3 About the fundamental value of crypto assets

With the emergence of a new asset class comes the difficulty of quantifying the fundamental, underlying value of these assets. For some, Bitcoin, the crypto asset with by far the highest market cap, is valueless comparing the crypto market with the tulip mania in the 17th century in the Netherlands. Microsoft founder Bill Gates, for example, describes Bitcoin as a pure "greater fool theory" type of investment, meaning that the Bitcoin hype is based on the buyers' belief that somebody will be willing to buy the asset at a higher price without considering the fundamental value (Cheng, 2018). For others, such as software pioneer John McAfee Bitcoin has fundamental value and one coin will be worth $1 million by 2020 (Nambiampurath, 2018). So how valuable is it really? The true value of Bitcoin is probably somewhere between the two extreme perceptions. Before diving into the different valuation models for crypto assets, the term "value" will be discussed in a broader way. What is the fundamental value of an asset in general? And how do crypto assets derive their value?

Wikipedia defines the fundamental value of an asset as follows: In finance, fundamental value (also: intrinsic value) refers to the value of a company, stock, currency or product determined through fundamental analysis without reference to its market value which is influenced by market conditions such as a recession or a speculative bubble. It is ordinarily calculated by summing the discounted future income generated by the asset to obtain the present value. It is worthy to note that this term may have different meanings for different assets" (Wikipedia, n.d.).

First of all, it is important to note that the fundamental value of an asset and the market value, which is reflected by the market price, need to be distinguished. The market price is very often driven by psychological factors. Especially in the crypto space many investors make decisions based on the behavior of other market participants, rather than hard analysis. Also, positive media coverage is one of the main factors driving the market price (Cameron & Trinh, 2017). All these factors are part of the extrinsic value of an asset and need to be excluded from a fundamental value analysis.

Furthermore, it is important to determine from what perspective it is looked at the value of a crypto asset. One could for example assess the value of a token at an ICO from an issuer's perspective or from a regulatory perspective with respect to financial reporting standards (IFRS). For the purpose of this thesis the token's value is viewed from a rational long-term investor's perspective. There are basically two motivations of investors that buy tokens. There are buyers who purchase a token in order to get access to the (future) utility of the token. Second, there are buyers that anticipate an in crease in the token's value and are looking for return on investment (D'Onorio Demeo & Young, 2017, p. 6).

Generally speaking, the value of a token is based on a combination of the purpose of the token and the underlying rights the holder has. For cryptocurrencies value is derived from strong features as a medium of exchange, store of value and unit of account. Especially, the ability to provide a monetary store of value to investors can drive a token's value to a great extent. This is especially the case for Bitcoin that is often discussed as the "digital gold". The value of a utility token is mainly derived from its usability. A good example is Ethereum, the second biggest crypto asset in terms of market cap, that derives its value from providing developers access to its virtual machine where they can build other tokens ("ERC-20 tokens") and decentralized apps ("dapps") on. For cryptocurrencies as well as utility tokens also, network effects play an important role which means the bigger the network gets the higher the value. Whereas the value of security tokens can be compared to the value of securities such as stocks that derive their value from future cash flow expectations. For asset backed tokens the value is theoretically equal to the value of the underlying asset (Hahn & Wons, 2018, p. 14).

4. Conceptual framework: Valuation techniques of crypto assets

The valuation of crypto assets is about determining the fundamental value of the asset regardless of the current market price. This helps to get a feeling for whether a token is over- or undervalued. It is comparable to fundamental analysis of traditional financial assets such as stocks. In traditional fundamental analysis for stocks financial reports help to calculate the value of a stock. This does not work for crypto assets anymore and new valuation techniques need to be developed in order to assess the monetary value of crypto assets.

A number of authors and leading thinkers in the crypto space have written about the valuation of crypto assets and have developed a wide range of valuation techniques that will be presented in the following pages. However, research is still its infancy as crypto assets themselves and it will take a few years until highly sophisticated and validated valuation models for this emerging asset class will be available. Historically, this is comparable to the development of valuation techniques for stocks which have been established decades after the first stock trading. While Dutch East India Co became the first company to offer its shares on a public exchange in the early 1600s, it was not until the 20th century that a comprehensive framework for calculating the fundamental value of equity securities was developed (Evans, 2018).

In general, there are two approaches of how to value a token or any other traditional asset class: absolute and relative valuation models. Absolute valuation models attempt to determine the absolute fundamental value, often referred to as the intrinsic value, for an asset. Such models are used to calculate an estimate of value that can be compared with the asset's market price. In traditional finance the absolute value of equities is usually calculated based on future returns that the investor expects to receive from holding the asset. A very common absolute model is the discounted cash flow model (DCF) (Henry, et al., 2010, p. 18). When it comes to absolute valuation models for crypto assets market sizing techniques, especially the Equation of Exchange based on the Quantity Theory of Money, has gotten the most traction in the market. But also, the asset rotation theory and the cost of production approach can help to estimate an absolute value for a crypto asset and therefore fall under the category of absolute valuation techniques.

On the other side, relative valuation models provide an estimate for the asset's value relative to that of another asset. The underlying idea of relative valuation models is that similar assets should be sold at similar prices. Relative valuation is usually conducted by calculating ratios. In traditional equity valuation the stock price is usually divided by a fundamental such as cash flow per share. The most common ratio for stocks is the price-to-earnings ratio (P/E ratio), which is the ratio of a stock's market price to the company's earnings per share. A stock with a relatively low P/E ratio is relatively undervalued (Henry, et al., 2010, p. 20). For crypto assets the most common relative metric is the Network Value-to-Transaction ratio (NVT ratio) that compares the network value (equals the market cap) of a token to the network's daily on-chain transaction volume.

In the following pages, the most common valuation techniques for crypto assets will be briefly explained. The aim is also to assess the usability of every valuation model for the different crypto asset categories, namely utility tokens, security tokens, cryptocurrencies and asset backed tokens. Furthermore, the limitations of the presented frameworks will be discussed. It should be noted that the valuation models are not to be used as a justification for investment but can be helpful to understand what factors are driving the value of a crypto asset. Beside to the fundamental quantitative analysis of crypto assets qualitative analysis such as the assessment of the quality of the team, the underlying technology, the community and developers or the white paper of the crypto project is crucial when it comes to the investment in crypto assets. However, the qualitative assessment of crypto assets is not subject of this thesis.

4.1 Discounted Cash Flow (DCF) and CAPM

First, one could think about using traditional valuation methodologies for assessing the value of crypto assets. This approach does not "reinvent the wheel" and looks at some very basic models from traditional finance and discusses how they could be applied to crypto assets. The basic traditional valuation model is the Discounted Cash Flow (DCF) model which derives the value of an investment from the discounted value of its expected future cash flows. For common stocks dividends are the usual form of cash flow. The following formula expresses the DCF model (Henry, et al., 2010, p. 85):

$$V_0 = \sum_{t=1}^{n} \frac{CF_t}{(1+r)^t}$$

with,
V_0 = present value of the asset
n = number of cash flows in the life of the asset
CF_t = expected cash flow at time t
r = discount rate or required rate of return

The discount rate r reflects the degree of risk of the investment. Alternatively, the required rate of return resulting from the Capital Asset Pricing Model (CAPM) could be used as an input for r. The CAPM formula looks as follows:

$$R_i = r_f + \beta_i (r_m - r_f)$$

with,
r_f = risk free rate
β_i = beta of the investment
r_m = expected market return
$(r_m - r_f)$ = risk premium

The CAPM formula is used to calculate the expected return on an investment. It is based on the assumption that an investor needs to be compensated for the time value of money (represented by the risk-free rate) and the systematic risk, also called non-diversifiable risk (represented by the risk premium). Beta is the investment's volatility relative to the overall market (Henry, et al., 2010, p. 57).

So how could these models be useful for crypto asset valuation. Most of the existing tokens do not offer any cash flow. However, there are some exceptions to which the original form of the DCF formula could theoretically be applied. As already explained, security tokens can have similar characteristics to traditional securities such as equities (stocks). In case they pay the investor dividend-like returns the DCF model is applicable to this kind of tokens. In addition, there are some staking and masternode tokens (such as NEO or VeChain) that guarantee the investor certain payments as a reward for holding the token that are used to validate transactions. These rewards could also be discounted to calculate the present value of an investment.

If somebody would like to apply the DCF model to other tokens than security tokens and proof-of-stake tokens formula needs to be adjusted slightly. Utility tokens provide a value to the investor based on a certain utility, which could be file storage, identity validation or supply chain trackability. Hence, one could estimate the value of future utility and discount it back to the present. These estimates for the future value replace the cash flows in the DCF formula (McKeon, 2017):

$$V_0 = \sum_{t=1}^{n} \frac{VF_t}{(1+r)^t}$$

with,
VF_t = expected flow of value at time t
Anything else as in the original formula

The prediction of the future value can be based on a top-down or bottom-up analysis of the future market. In the top-down approach, one would start with the total size of the addressable market and then estimate what percentage of that market can be captured by a certain token. In the bottom-up approach, one would start with the existing market size of the token and make assumptions on the rate of growth of that market. Sometimes a combination of these approaches could be useful (Kalla, 2017). Of course, this might be very sensitive to subjective assumptions. Another difficult task is to find a reasonable discount rate. Generally, it should represent the high risk of crypto asset investments. Discount rates of at least 30-50%, similar to high-risk venture capital stocks, seem to be accurate.

Another possibility is the calculation of a required rate of return based on a crypto adjusted CAPM. The expected market return (r_m) could be calculated based on the historical data of the whole crypto asset market. However, it becomes more difficult when it comes to the risk-free rate (r_f) and beta ($β_i$). Due to the immature state of the crypto market reliable variables cannot be calculated (yet). The fixed returns that an investor receives when holding proof-of-stake tokens could potentially serve as the risk-free rate. But there is absolutely no certainty that these tokens will still exist in a couple of years, which makes the going concern assumption invalid. Until now, it also makes no sense to calculate a beta for single crypto assets due to the extremely high volatility and dependency of all altcoins to Bitcoin. However, there have been attempts to calculate the beta of Bitcoin relative to portfolios of other asset classes (e.g. Bitcoin vs. S&P 500). Some authors even suggest to include completely new inputs into a "crypto CAPM" such as momentum/"FOMO", community strength or economic/political uncertainty factors that all have significant impact on the expected rate of return of crypto assets (Lannquist, 2018). It will be interesting to see how research in this field will develop. The more the crypto market matures the more reliable date will be available to establish a meaningful CAPM for crypto assets.

4.2 Asset rotation theory

The asset rotation theory is probably the simplest approach of crypto asset valuation. The idea simply assumes that certain proportions of capital will flow out of traditional assets into crypto assets because they might offer better features and are uncorrelated with traditional asset classes (McKeon, 2017).

It could, for example, be assumed that 10% of the total gold value will rotate to Bitcoin by the year 2020. According to the World Gold Council, the total value of all gold ever mined is about $7.8 trillion (World Gold Council, n.d.). The total Bitcoin supply as of prediction date will be roughly 18 million. Simple math results in a stored value per Bitcoin of approximately $43,300 (= (10% x $7.8 trillion) / 18 million BTC). The same logic could be applied to foreign exchange or stock markets.

The question is why should people move investment capital from gold to Bitcoin? Proponents of the asset rotation idea often refer to Bitcoin as the "digital gold". They see many similarities between the two assets. People value gold because of trust that is based on its history even though it doesn't have much functional usability (except jewelry and some industry usage). Therefore, people can value Bitcoin in the same way. Second, the supply of gold as well as of Bitcoin is not centrally controlled, and they can't be inflated by politicians. There is a fixed amount of gold in the world and a maximum of 21 million Bitcoins (Samani, 2017a). In addition, both can be used as a hedge against the risk of fiat currency inflation. In some countries, such as Venezuela or Zimbabwe the fear of hyperinflation is real, and people already start to move their money into Bitcoin (Urban, 2017). In some points Bitcoin is even superior then gold since it is easier to store, more secure and better divisible. Of course, there are also many arguments against Bitcoin as the digital gold. A frequent claim is that the gold price is not as volatile as Bitcoin, what makes gold a more stable store of value. This is true today, but it can be expected that Bitcoin's volatility decreases with an increasing market cap because of lower impacts of capital flows on the market. When Bitcoin is worth $1 trillion, $10 billion capital flows will move the market far less than a $10 billion capital flow would relative to current network value of around $100 billion. Other benefits of gold are its history over thousands of years that created trust among people, its physical nature as well as the fact that it is generally easier to understand than Bitcoin. However, in the last decades the raise of modern technologies has shown that these arguments can become meaningless in a fast-changing world. The internet, for example, is non-physical and was not understandable to the general public decades ago but people accepted it in their daily lives exceptionally fast (Samani, 2017a).

The asset rotation theory seems to be logic and provides a rough idea where capital that is invested in crypto assets is coming from. But the idea is generally too simple and not helpful in order to calculate an exact fundamental value for certain crypto assets. The theory is not scientifically proven, and nobody knows if asset rotation from gold to Bitcoin is already taking place. There is currently no reliable data on this topic. And even if one believes in the asset rotation theory it is still unclear how the rotating capital flows into different crypto assets, since it cannot be assumed that all the capital will be invested into Bitcoin. Finally, the theory only makes sense if it is applied to crypto assets that serve as a store of value. It could maybe also be used for security tokens, for example, under the assumption that a certain portion of capital invested in stocks will move to equity tokens. However, for utility tokens it is rather an unsuitable tool to explain value drivers.

4.3 Equation of Exchange (Quantity Theory of Money)

The Equation of Exchange, based on the Quantity Theory of Money, is the valuation model that has attracted the most attention in the crypto space. The macroeconomic model was originally published by the economist Irving Fisher in his book *The Purchasing Power of Money* in the year 1911 and was originally developed to analyze the functioning of fiat money in an economy. The original Equation of Exchange looks as follows (Weber, 2018):

$$MV = PQ$$

with,
M = total quantity of money in circulation on average in an economy
V = velocity of money, the average frequency with which a unit of money is spent
P = price level of products and services in an economy
Q = quantity of all products and services in an economy

The left side of the formula represents the money supply (M) that is needed to serve the money demand (PQ) in a specific economy at a certain velocity (V). Traditionally PQ represents the gross domestic product of a country by multiplying the price level per unit of output and the quantity of units of output (Weber, 2018). The following example explains the formula in a very simple way: Imagine a mini economy where 10 apples, that are worth 2 dollars each, are sold per year. PQ, which represents the GDP of that mini economy, is then 20 dollars (10 apples × $2). The velocity V is defined as the frequency at which one unit of money is spent in a given period (usually one year) (Burniske & Tatar, 2018, p. 178). Assuming that in this mini economy one-dollar changes hands 5 times per year, a total money supply (M) of only 4 dollars would be required to serve the mini economy (M = PQ/V = $20/5 = 4). Of course, this is an oversimplified example but it illustrates the underlying idea of the Equation of Exchange very well.

Chris Burniske, a leading crypto analyst, was the first author who applied a variation of Fisher's theory to crypto assets. The basic idea is that every token is serving a specific token economy as a currency. Burniske rearranged the formula by solving it for M (Burniske, 2017):

$$M = PQ/V$$

with,
M = size of the monetary base
V = velocity of the token
P = price of the digital resource being provisioned, and
Q = quantity of the digital resource being provisioned.

M represents the size of the monetary base which means the size of token supply (market cap of a token) necessary to support a crypto-economy of size PQ, at Velocity V (Burniske, 2017).

The multiplication of P and Q represents the token GDP which can be understood as a mini economy served by the token. It is important to note that P is not representing the token price, but rather the price of the resource being provisioned by the crypto network. For example, in the case of Filecoin, which is a token that enables online data storage, P would be the price per gigabyte (GB) of storage provisioned, measured in $/GB. Q represents the quantity of that resource provisioned, in the case of Filecoin the GBs of storage. In general, PQ can just be defined as the total value of the token economy, similar to the gross domestic product (GDP) of a country. The current PQ of a token is represented by the annual on-chain transaction volume of the token, even though the number is distorted by transactions that are not part of the real token economy (such as transactions between exchanges). Looking at the GDP of nation states, FX volume is not incorporated neither (Burniske, 2017).

The velocity V is defined as the number of times a token changes hands in a given period (usually one year). Bitcoin, for example, processed an average of $160 million in transaction value per day in 2016, summing up to $58 billion per year (=PQ). The average Bitcoin market cap through 2016 was $8.9 billion (=M). This results in a velocity of 6.5 (= $58 bn / $8.9 bn). A velocity of 6.5 means that in 2016 each Bitcoin changed hands 6.5 times in average. In reality, a small percentage of Bitcoin in the float likely changed hands much more than that, whereas a larger portion was stored and did never change hands (Burniske, 2017). For comparison only, the velocity of the USD M1 money stock is about 5.5 at the time of writing (FRED, 2018)

After defining all variables of the formula, the Equation of Exchange can help to value a token by conducting the following steps:

1. Estimate the future total addressable market (TAM) of the token
2. Determine the future token economy (PQ) by defining potential percent penetration of the TAM
3. Estimate the future velocity V of the token
4. Calculate the monetary base M necessary to support PQ with M = PQ/V
5. Divide the monetary base by the total numbers of tokens issued
6. Discount the future utility value to the present (Burniske, 2017)

The steps will be briefly explained by the example of Bitcoin. Keep In mind, that this is a brief walkthrough that helps to grasp the theory. The model will be treated in more detail in the practical part of this thesis within the valuation of the IOTA token. So first, a total addressable market (TAM) analysis needs to be conducted, which is also typically used in traditional finance for analyzing the potential of startup companies. To value Bitcoin, it can be assumed that Bitcoin will have two major use cases: international remittances and store of value as "digital gold". Burniske argues that a token's value is additive depending on the number of use cases it serves. Of course, Bitcoin could have other use cases such as online payments for e-commerce or others. For reasons of simplicity only two use cases are considered. **Table 1** shows the estimated total market volumes, the Bitcoin market share as well as the velocity in the year 2025:

	Total market estimate 2025 (bn $)	Bitcoin market share (%)	Bitcoin market share (bn $)	Estimated velocity	Required monetary base M (bn $)
Remittances	750	20%	150	5	30
Sore of value (digital gold)	7.800	10%	780	1	780

Table 1: Bitcoin target markets and required monetary base in 2025 (World Gold Council, n.d.; Burniske 2018)

The estimate of the total remittances market volume in 2025 is taken from Burniske's book *Cryptoassets* (Burniske & Tatar, 2018, p. 181). The estimate for the global gold market equals the total value of all gold ever mined which will probably not change significantly until 2025 (World Gold Council, n.d.). In the remittances the Bitcoin velocity is assumed to be 5 in 2025, similar to the current Bitcoin velocity. Holding Bitcoin as "digital gold" results in a velocity of 1 since Bitcoin is just being held as an investment. This results in a total required monetary base M of $810 billion (= $30 bn + $780 bn). The approximate number of Bitcoins issued in the year 2025 will be 20 million. Dividing $810 billion by 20 million results in $40,500 which means that every Bitcoin would need to store $40,500 of value to meet the demand of 20 percent of global remittances and 10% of the gold market. This number represents the future utility value of Bitcoin in the year 2025 (Burniske & Tatar, 2018, p. 179).

At this point another key concept of Burniske's valuation model needs to be applied: Discount rates. Analysts use discounting to figure out how much they should pay for something now if it is expected to be worth more in the future. In the traditional DCF model future cash flows are usually discounted, whereas in crypto asset valuation rather the future utility value needs to be discounted. The discount rate should reflect the risk associated to the investment. For crypto assets 30-50% are commonly used as a discount rate which is comparable to high risk venture capital projects. So, discounting the hypothetical future value of $40,500 per Bitcoin with a rate of 30% over 7 years results in a present value of around $6,450 (Burniske & Tatar, 2018, p. 179 f.). As of the date of writing the market price of Bitcoin is about $7,500 which means that the Bitcoin price is slightly overvalued.

According to Burniske the token value consists of two components: The "current utility value" (CUV) which represents the value driven by current usage of the token, and a "discounted expected utility value" (DEUV), which represents value driven by expected future utility discounted back to the present. When a token is first launched, DEUV dominates the token's value. CUV steadily grows, the more the token gets adopted. Ultimately in the steady state, CUV should drive token price (Lannquist, 2018). According to Burniske having more than 20% in current utility value is currently very unusual in the crypto space, as many crypto projects don't have a product adopted on market yet (Burniske, 2017).

The Equation of Exchange seem to be a valuation model that is mainly applicable to utility tokens that serve as an access to a specific ecosystem. By quantifying the future total value of this token economy, the model can be helpful to calculate the expected utility value of the token. The model is also suitable for cryptocurrencies that serve as a medium of exchange or store of value, as seen in the Bitcoin example. However, the model seems to be unsuitable neither for security tokens nor for asset backed tokens since they generally do not create or serve a specific token economy.

Even though the model seems to be extremely thoughtful it has a few drawbacks. In general, the model is very sensitive to its input parameters such as the velocity, the future market volume or the discount rate, which makes it easy to be manipulated. A common comment about such models is "garbage in, garbage out", in other words the model is only as good as the assumptions are and these assumptions can vary widely among investors. Especially the velocity is a crucial input parameter of the model. Slight changes in the estimation of the velocity change the outcome to a big extent. Unfortunately, velocity is hard to measure and nearly impossible to predict in the future. Another critic is that velocity is used as an independent input parameter rather than estimating it along with its interdependency to other variables.

The model reveals another issue related to the velocity, that is very often subject of valuation discussions in the crypto space. Many big market participants such as one of the biggest crypto news platform CoinDesk have published articles about the "velocity problem". Due to the syntax of the Equation of Exchange formula ($M = PQ/V$) the model implies that the higher the velocity, the lower the token value, all else equal. This has led to the perplexing assumption that the more a token is used for utility purposes (which results in a higher velocity), the lower the token value. This is very often described as a big risk for many utility tokens that do not have the purpose of storing value (Samani, 2017b). Many teams behind utility tokens are taking this issue seriously by looking for ways how to motivate investors to hold a portion of tokens which leads in a reduction of velocity. Some project designers implemented features that force velocity reductions, such as staking functions (e.g. FunFair) or balanced burn-and-mint mechanics (e.g. Factom) (Lannquist, 2018). However, from a mathematical point of view, it is not correct to say: The higher the token's velocity, the lower it's value. Simple calculations prove that this is only the case if velocity increases faster then the token's GDP as illustrated in the following:

Scenario A: $r_{PQ} = r_V$

Time	PQ (GDP)	Growth rate PQ	V (Velocity)	Growth rate V	M (= PQ/V)
1	100,0	10%	5	10%	20
2	110,0	10%	5,5	10%	20
3	121,0	10%	6,1	10%	20
4	133,1	10%	6,7	10%	20
5	146,4	10%	7,3	10%	20

Scenario B: $r_{PQ} > r_V$

Time	PQ (GDP)	Growth rate PQ	V (Velocity)	Growth rate V	M (= PQ/V)
1	100,0	10%	5	5%	20,0
2	110,0	10%	5,3	5%	21,0
3	121,0	10%	5,5	5%	22,0
4	133,1	10%	5,8	5%	23,0
5	146,4	10%	6,1	5%	24,1

Scenario C: $r_{PQ} < r_V$

Time	PQ (GDP)	Growth rate PQ	V (Velocity)	Growth rate V	M (= PQ/V)
1	100,0	10%	5	20%	20,0
2	110,0	10%	6,0	20%	18,3
3	121,0	10%	7,2	20%	16,8
4	133,1	10%	8,6	20%	15,4
5	146,4	10%	10,4	20%	14,1

Table 2: PQV growth ratio (r_{PQ}/r_V) (own creation)

The three tables show different scenarios to illustrate how the relation of the growth rates of the token GDP (r_{PQ}) and the velocity (r_V) influence the token value. It can be seen that if the growth rates equal ($r_{PQ} = r_V$) the token value remains the same (scenario A). If the token GDP grows faster than the velocity ($r_{PQ} > r_V$) the token appreciates in value (scenario B). Only if the velocity growth outpaces the growth of the token GDP ($r_{PQ} < r_V$) the monetary base M decreases, and so the token value. These findings could be condensed in a formula, let's call it the PQV growth ratio:

$$PQV\ growth\ ratio = r_{PQ}/r_V$$

If > 1: increasing token value
If = 1: stagnating token value
If < 1: decreasing token value

The continuous calculation of the PQV growth ratio could help investors that are interested in an increase of the token value to make investment decisions. The historical PQV growth ratio should be calculable for most of the existing tokens since it is based on the token's past total transaction volume (PQ) and past velocity (V).

Finally, some critics also argue that the model is mainly based on speculations. Indeed, especially for tokens that were just launched the value is mainly derived from future utility. However, the model takes the risk into consideration by discounting the calculated future utility value. Moreover, it needs to be noted that also traditional valuation models such as the DCF model are based on expected future returns.

All in all, the model has fair critics, and even Chris Burniske admit its drawbacks by saying that he is "not convinced MV = PQ will remain the cornerstone to crypto asset valuation and that he is open and excited to see other equations and frameworks" (Bruniske, 2018)

4.4 Network Value to Transaction (NVT) ratio

The Network Value to Transactions (NVT) ratio is a relative valuation metric that was introduced and popularized by Willy Woo, Chris Burniske and the Cryptometric team. The NVT ratio is similar to the popular Price-to-Earnings ratio (P/E Ratio) in traditional stock valuation, hence often referred to as the "crypto P/E ratio". The traditional P/E ratio is simply the stock's market price divided by the company's earnings per share. A stock with a low P/E ratio, relatively to the P/E of another comparable stock, is considered a relatively undervalued (a good buy). On the other hand, a stock with a relatively high P/E, is considered as relatively overvalued or a company of high growth (Henry, et al., 2010, p. 20). For crypto assets the price is represented by the network value which represents the total market value of all tokens in circulation. Tokens usually do not have earnings similar to stocks (this might change with the emergence of security tokens). However, since most of the tokens can be seen as a payments network, the money flowing through the network can be considered as an equivalent to "company earnings". The transaction volume is a proxy for fundamental utility value of the network (Woo, 2017). Hence, the formula for the NVT ratio looks as follows:

$$\text{NVT ratio} = \frac{\text{Network value}}{\text{Daily transaction volume}}$$

with,

Network value = market cap of a token

Daily transaction volume = daily on-chain transaction volume (trading volume excluded)

At its essence, the NVT ratio is "a comparison of how much the network is being valued to how much the network is being used" (Woo, 2017). A high NVT ratio indicates that its network valuation is outpacing the value being transmitted on its network. This can happen when the network is in high growth and investors are valuing it as a high return investment, or alternatively when the price is in an unsustainable bubble (Woo, 2018).

Until now, the NVT ratio has been widely used to assess the value of a token by comparing the actual NVT ratio to the historical development of the NVT ratio, rather than comparing it to the NVT ratio of other tokens. Willy Woo argues that a trend analysis of Bitcoin's NVT ratio can help to detect bubbles, as shown in **Figure 2**:

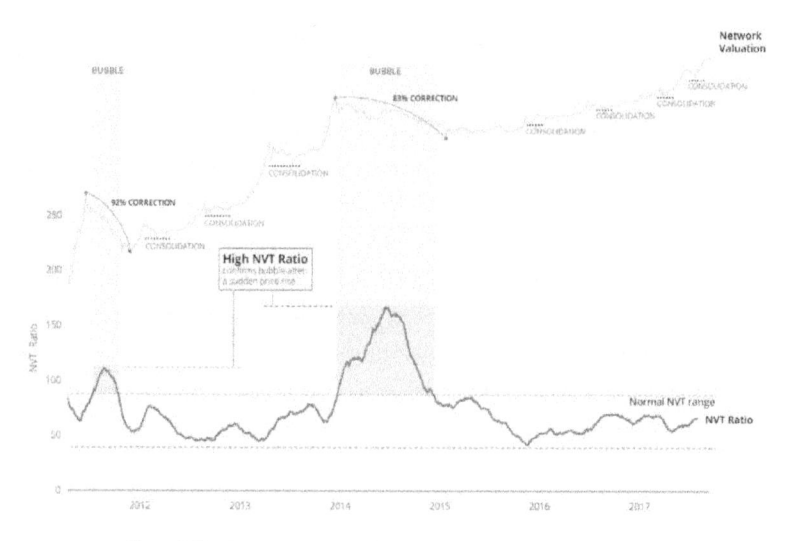

Figure 3: Bitcoin network value and NVT ratio from 2012 to 2017 (Woo, 2017)

In 2011 and early 2013, Bitcoin exploded in price followed by NVT ratio rising above the normal range. These were identified as bubbles under NVT ratio analysis. Subsequently there were lengthy 92% and 83% corrections in price (Woo, 2017).

However, critics argue that the course of the NVT ratio follows the bubble with a delay of a few months weakening its indicative and predictive power. By looking at the graph the critic seems to be fair enough since the peak of the NVT coincides with the middle of a correction period. That's why the NVT in this form cannot be used as an indicator for overvaluation or a bubble (Kalichkin, 2018a). This is the reason why different crypto analysts such as Dmitry Kalichkin started to experiment with moving averages of the input parameters of the NVT ratio. They came to the conclusion that the optimal solution is to divide daily Network Value by 90-day moving average of transaction volume. The formula of the refined NVT ratio looks as follows (Kalichkin, 2018a):

$$NVT_{new} = \frac{\text{Daily NV}}{90 \text{ MA (Daily TV)}}$$

There is a quite logical reason for the fact that a moving average of the daily transaction volume in the dominator leads to better results. Usually strong price increases go hand in hand with higher trading activities on exchanges (off-chain transactions). This is shorty followed by an increasing on-chain transaction volume since many investors want to liquidate their positions. Exchanges and wallets start to exchange funds on-chain to provide this liquidity to investors. This transaction volume is entirely speculation-driven and does not represent fundamental utility value of the network. Due to this fact transaction volume follows the price. By using a 90-day moving average of the transaction volume (denominator of the NVT ratio) this reflexivity of the transaction volume is eliminated, and the time lag found in the old NVT formula is removed (Kalichkin, 2018a).

As you can see in the following the refined NVT ratio based on a 90-day moving average of the transaction volume produces much more responsive charts that can serve as a value indicator of crypto assets, in this case Bitcoin **(Figure 4 and 5)**:

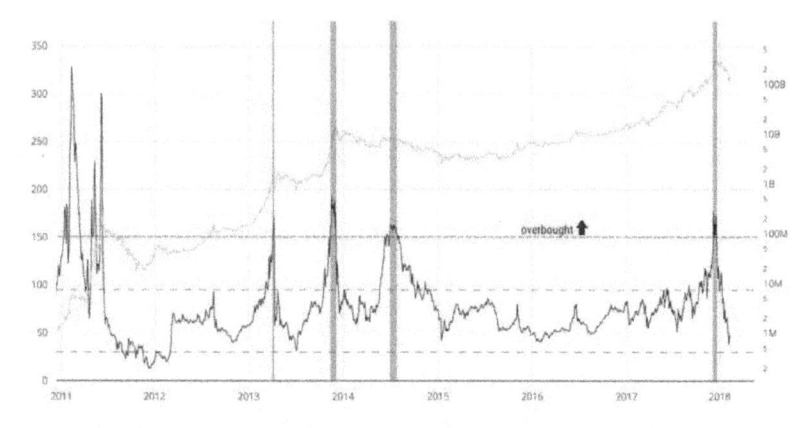

Figure 4: Bitcoin network value and refined NVT ratio – overvaluation (Kalichkin, 2018a)

For Bitcoin, any NVT ratio above 150 is an indicator of potential overvaluation and a sign of a bubble, marked in red in the graph (overbought zone).

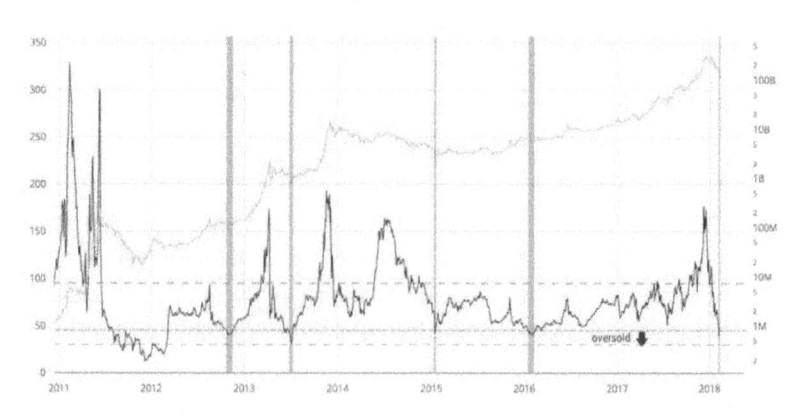

Figure 5: Bitcoin network value and refined NVT ratio – undervaluation (Kalichkin, 2018a)

A Bitcoin NVT ratio below 45 indicates potential undervaluation and could be a good buy opportunity of the token. You can observe this in green bars in **Figure 5** (Woo, 2018). However, these findings could not be generalized. In an analysis of Litecoin's refined NVT over time it could be observed that the NVT ratio spiked several times, while the price kept increasing. Those cases can usually be explained by a strong trend or some big external news, that should always be taken into consideration in the analysis (Kalichkin, 2018a).

The NVT ratio generally suits all tokens whose on-chain transaction volume mainly represents the utility for the users. It is basically calculable for all tokens with a measurable network value and transaction volume. This is the case for most of the cryptocurrencies and utility tokens since public blockchains are usually transparent, so that their monetary throughput can be measured. However, many private tokens such Monero hide some, or all of their value transmitted on-chain so it's impossible to determine their NVT ratio accurately. But even if it is possible to calculate the NVT ratio, the majority of tokens is still not mature enough and it will take some time before their NVT ratio turns into a useful tool as a valuation metric.

Furthermore, a major problem of the NVT ratio is that the on-chain transaction volumes are inflated due to the existence of transactions that do not represent the fundamental utility of the token such as transactions made by exchanges, staking and mixer activities, spam etc. According to Coinmetrics transaction volumes are highly unreliable and may be overstated by a factor of 5-10 or more (Coinmetrics, 2018a). Fortunately, there are analysts, such as the Coinmetrics team, that are working on measuring the actual economic throughput of public blockchains in order to calculate adjusted NVT ratios. Currently, they are steadily calculating the NVT for over 50 tokens (Coinmetrics, 2018b).

Until now, it is also questionable to what extent the NVT ratio can be a framework for comparative analysis among different tokens. Currently it is mainly used as a valuation indicator based on the historical development of a single token. Tokens differ very much in their underlying technology and usability purpose. Also, it is still unclear how relevant on-chain transaction volume is across protocols. This makes it important to identify comparable crypto assets, a so-called peer group, in order to achieve a meaningful comparison of the NVT ratios between them.

4.5 Metcalfe's Law

Metcalfe's Law was published by the founder of the Ethernet Robert Metcalfe in the 1980s. The model originally intended to determine the value of any kind of telecommunication network consisting of devises such as fax machines, telephones etc. Metcalfe's Law stated that the value of a network is proportional to the square of the number of connected users in the system (n²), which is also described as the "network effect". The underlying idea is that a "network has little or no value with just one user, however with each new user, the utility value of the network more than doubles" (D'Onorio Demeo & Young, 2017, p. 16). Later research has shown that the theory could also be applied to social networks. The revenue of Facebook as well as of Tencent, China's largest social network, was proved to be proportional to the square of its monthly active users (MAU) (Zhang, et al., 2015). Recently, some researchers tried to use Metcalfe's Law for the valuation of crypto assets, resulting in the following formula (D'Onorio Demeo & Young, 2017, p. 11):

$$\text{Network value} = N^2 \times \text{transaction volume per user}$$

With,
N = number of daily active addresses (DAA) or number of daily transactions

According to the analyst Tom Lee "94% of the Bitcoin movement over the past four years can be explained by that equation" (Silverstein, 2017). However, as explained in the chapter before, transaction volume is very reflexive to price and should rather be smoothed by a 90-day average. Other critics state that Metcalfe's law tends to overvalue crypto assets. Therefore, some variations have been proposed, for example using $N^{1,5}$ or a log function (n × log n) as an input. Dmitry Kalichkin, a leading thinker in the field of crypto asset valuation, supposed to define the original Metcalfe's law (N^2) and the log function (n × log n) as upper and lower bounds for the value of crypto networks. Since Metcalfe's law tends to overvaluation it is logically used a the upper bound. Applying his idea to Bitcoin, results in quite meaningful findings (Kalichkin, 2018b):

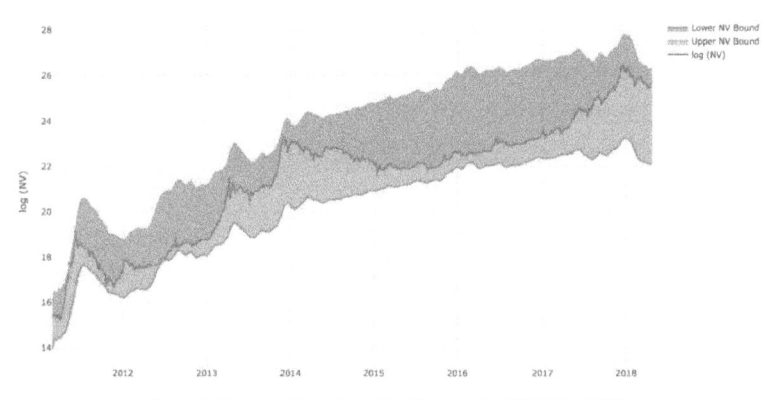

Figure 6: Upper and lower bound for Bitcoin value (Kalichkin, 2018b)

As **Figure 6** shows, the Bitcoin market value (represented by the bold green line) stays within these bounds derived from Metcalfe's original law and the log function. It can also be observed that every time Bitcoin's market value approaches the upper bound, there was a correction followed. On the other hand, whenever the market value was close to the lower bound it was a good investment opportunity (Kalichkin, 2018b).

Now, the upper and lower bounds could be put together by using the halfsum of both as a bottom-up valuation of the Bitcoin network as a function of DAA, resulting in the following graph (**Figure 7**) (Kalichkin, 2018b):

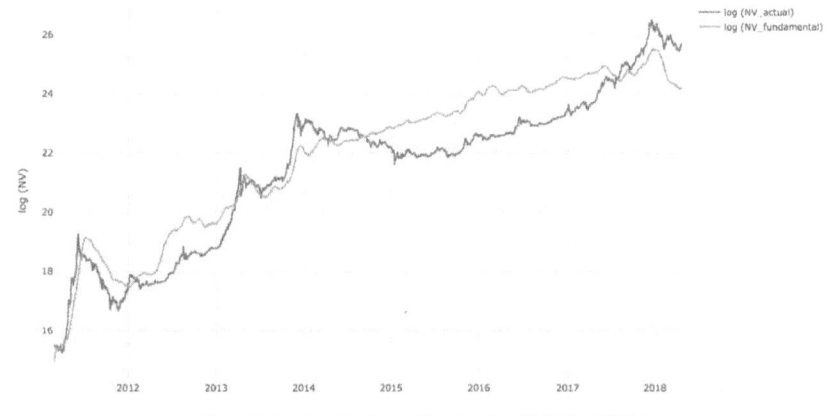

Figure 7: Actual and estimated Bitcoin value (Kalichkin, 2018b)

Every time the blue line, representing Bitcoin's market value, runs above the orange line, representing the valuation metric based on N^2 and (n × log n), this is an indicator for an overvaluation of Bitcoin, vise versa. According to the graph, Bitcoin is still overvalued as of the date of writing even after the extreme price decline in the last months (Kalichkin, 2018b).

In general, the Metcalfe's law can be an accurate valuation indicator. However, the basic form of the formula is not scientifically proven and cannot be universally applied to every token. It rather need to be adjusted based on the historical development of a token's performance. Different functions of network growth (such as N^2, $N^{1,5}$, n log(n) etc.) need to be evaluated in order to have a valuation formula that is indicative enough. The findings of this analysis can be different from token to token, maybe even inconclusive for some.

It needs to be emphasized that the valuation model only makes sense for network tokens whose utility value increases with the number of users. This might be the case for all cryptocurrencies as well as some utility tokens. The model is unsuitable for pure investment tokens that serve as a way to passively invest in an issuing entity or underlying asset (security token, asset backed tokens...).

4.6 Cost of production approach

The cost of production approach considers crypto assets as commodities that are products of a competitive mining market, rather than networks. Crypto analysts such as Tom Lee often refer to the production costs of Bitcoin as a value indicator. Recently, Lee stated that Bitcoin is currently undervalued comparing its market price of around $7,000 to its actual mining costs that are around the same level. According to him "Bitcoin has historically traded at 2.5 times its mining costs" (Belvedere, 2018).

Adam Hayes was the first author who introduced the cost of production model to Bitcoin. His main thesis is that the amount of mining (computational) power is the main driver of a token's value. Mining is generally referred to as the process of verifying and recording transactions into the distributed ledger (called "Proof of work") by using computational power, which is carried out by specific hardware and measured in hashes per second (hashrate). In the case of Bitcoin, the motivation of miners is the chance to earn newly created blocks of Bitcoins (Hayes, 2015, p. 2). The mining process is generally characterized by a very high electricity consumption which is the main cost factor in the generation of new Bitcoins. It might be interesting to note that Bitcoin would rank in the 41st place in the country ranking in terms of electricity consumption (Digiconomist, 2018).

According to Hayes somebody would only undertake mining if the marginal cost per day (electricity consumption) were less than or equal to the marginal product (the number of Bitcoins found per day on average multiplied by the dollar price of Bitcoin). Based on this assumption he defined the following formula for Bitcoin's fundamental value (Hayes, 2015, p. 13):

$$P^* = \frac{E_{day}}{BTC/day}$$

with E_{day} = (marginal) cost of production per day

The (marginal) cost of production per day, E_{day} per unit of mining power can be expressed as (Hayes, 2015, p. 12):

$$E_{day} = (\rho/1000)(\$/kWh \cdot WperGH/s \cdot hrs_{day})$$

with,
ρ = Hashpower (computational power) employed by a miner
$/kWh = USD price per kilowatt-hour
$WperGH/s$ = energy efficiency of the hardware
hrs_{day} = number of hours in a day

According to microeconomic theory, given a competitive market, the marginal product should equate with its marginal cost, which should also equal its selling price. In fact, Hayes defines P* as the lower bound for the token's value, below which a miner would operate at a marginal loss and therefore stops his mining activity (Hayes, 2018, p. 5).

So how could this model be used as a value indicator of Bitcoin? In an empirical analysis Hayes compared the ratio of Bitcoin's market price to the modeled price over time resulting in an average ratio of 1.05 and a standard deviation of $\sigma = 0.33$, which is incredibly accurate. The findings are illustrated in the following graph (**Figure 8**):

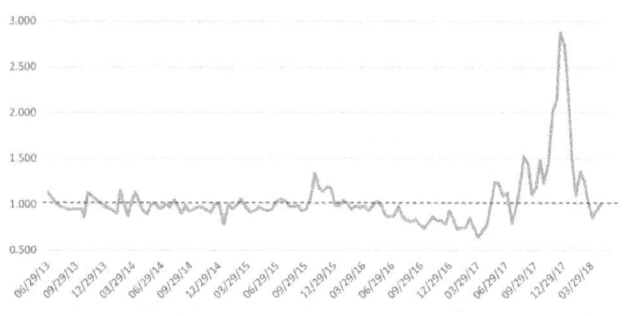

Figure 8: Ratio of Bitcoin market price to model price (Hayes, 2018)

A ratio of 1 would indicate that the two values are identical, anything over 1 indicates an overvaluation of Bitcoin's market price. The market price seems to fluctuate around the modeled price, except from September 2017 through January 2018, where there was a huge overvaluation of Bitcoin. This was followed by a correction of the market price to the modeled price based on the production costs. It is also important to note that the market price never dropped significantly below the modeled price, which supports the assumption that the production costs serve as the lower bound of the Bitcoin's value and that the value will never collapse to zero (Hayes, 2018, p. 6).

However, this leaves the question of causality. Is the market price determining the production costs or the other way around? Hayes applied a Granger test typically used to suggest temporal causality confirming the hypothesis that the model price market does "cause" the market price. According to Hayes this validates the predictive power of the cost of production model (Hayes, 2018, p. 9).

Despite Hayes analysis, critics doubt the causality assumption that the market value follows the production costs of Bitcoin. They argue that Bitcoin's market value determines the mining difficulty in the Bitcoin algorithm which affects the production costs (Sams, 2014). More research is to be made in this discussion. Since, the model only considers the production side and disregards other value drivers such as market prospects, it might be a tool that is more useful for miners, rather than for investors. It can help miners to calculate mining profitability and identify the breakeven point. However, investors could take the model into consideration in order to figure out the bottom level of a token value. Finally, the model has only been applied to Bitcoin. It would be interesting to see the usability for other tokens such as Ethereum. But the model is definitely only applicable to mineable (proof-of-work) tokens and can't help to determine the value of tokens that don't have any production costs such as the IOTA token.

4.7 Accessibility discount

The concept of the accessibility discount is very often underestimated by investors of crypto assets, even though it cannot serve as a comprehensive valuation model. The basic idea is that most of the crypto assets are traded under their value, if their accessibility to investors is limited. Limited accessibility in this context means that an investment in a crypto asset is difficult due to regulatory or operational obstacles such as no or very few listings of the asset on crypto exchanges. Especially newly issued tokens are very often characterized by huge accessibility discounts. It could be observed that the price of such tokens appreciated very much after listings on one of the big crypto exchanges (e.g. Binance, Coinbase or Bitfinex) (Paul, 2017). This is comparable to the index effect on traditional stock markets implying that firms included in the S&P 500 index usually experience an appreciation in value (Kasch & Sarkar, 2011).

In the following graph you can see the price rally of the cryptocurrency Monero after the South Korean crypto exchange Bithumb announced the listing of the token on August 21st, 2017:

Figure 9: Monero price appreciation after Bithumb listing (CoinMarketCap, 2018)

Figure 9 shows that the price of Monero almost doubled within several hours. The tremendous price increase was supported by the fact that Monero was not traded at all on Asian exchanges before. Similar price appreciations were experiences after the addition of Litecoin or Bitcoin Cash to Coinbase, the largest crypto exchange in the USA.

Accessibility can also be looked at from an institutional perspective. Currently there are still very high obstacles for institutions such as banks or foundations to invest in crypto assets, so that it can be assumed that there is still a huge accessibility discount. One obstacle for institutional investors is the lack of qualified custodial services of third parties (e.g. custodian banks) that can serve as an intermediate between the institutional investor and the crypto market. Another obstacle is the absence of institutional investment vehicles such as ETF's (exchange-traded fund). Experts estimate that, for example, an index ETF that represents the 10 largest crypto assets issued by a bulge bracket bank could collect at least $100 billion investment capital within one year (Paul, 2017). It can be expected that the obstacles for institutional investors will be removed more and more. Recently, the US crypto exchange Coinbase opened a custodian service targeting institutional Investors (Huillet, 2018) and Europe's largest trader of exchange-traded funds (ETFs) is also entering the crypto world (Shen, 2018).

Even though, it can certainly be assumed that the price of a token appreciates the easier it gets to buy it, it is very hard to quantify the accessibility discount and put it into a valuation framework. The concept does not give as a price target saying "crypto asset XY is worth $Z" but investors should definitely consider the accessibility of a crypto asset and ask the following questions: What percentage of people that want to buy the asset are currently able to buy it? What catalysts will make it more accessible? How probable will these catalysts take place?

4.8 Key findings

The following overview (**Table 3**) sums up all key findings of the theoretical part of this thesis. It illustrates how the different valuation models consider crypto assets (investment, currency, network or product). It also shows to which token types the different models can be applied to:

Valuation model	sees crypto assets as…	applicable to…
Original DCF and CAPM	Investment	Tokens with fixed returns (e.g. security or staking tokens)
Adjusted DCF and CAPM	Investment	All tokens (when models are mature enough)
Asset rotation theory	Investment	All tokens
Equation of Exchange	Currency	Cryptocurrencies, utility tokens
NVT ratio	Network	Network tokens (cryptocurrencies, some utility tokens)
Metcalfe's Law	Network	Network tokens (cryptocurrencies, some utility tokens)
Cost of production approach	Product, commodity	Mineable tokens with production costs
Accessibility discount	Investment	All tradable tokens

Table 3: Key findings – conceptual part (own creation)

5. Case application: Valuation of the IOTA token

This section is supposed to apply one of the previously presented valuation models to one specific crypto asset, namely the IOTA token. The first subchapter introduces the reader to the IOTA's vision, its underlying technology and brief history. The second subchapter tries to determine the current fundamental value of the IOTA token based on the Equation of Exchange.

5.1 About IOTA

IOTA is an open source distributed ledger technology (DLT) that is designed to be the backbone of the machine economy and Internet of Things (IoT). The number of connected devices worldwide is estimated to reach 75 billion by 2025. IOTA is aiming to provide a secure and decentralized environment to transfer data and settle feeless payments with the IOTA token among these devises. To achieve this, IOTA goes "beyond blockchain" by using a newly invented protocol called 'the Tangle', which is supposed to overcome the major limitations of the blockchain such as fees and scalability (IOTA Foundation, 2018).

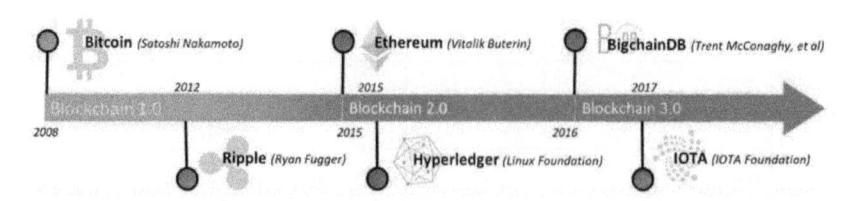

Figure 10: Development of DLT protocols from 2012 to 2017 (IOTA Foundation, 2018)

Due to the groundbreaking features of IOTA, it is often referred to as blockchain 3.0 or 3rd generation blockchain (see **Figure 10**), even though technically seen its underlying distributed ledger technology, the Tangle, is not a blockchain. **Figure 11** illustrates the different structure of the IOTA Tangle compared to a traditional blockchain, which is the basis of most crypto assets such as Bitcoin or Ethereum (IOTA Foundation, 2018):

Blockchain   Tangle (DAG/ Directed Acyclic Graph)

Figure 11: Illustration of blockchain vs. IOTA Tangle (IOTA Foundation, 2018)

The Tangle is a so-called Directed Acyclic Graph (DAG). In contrast to blockchain, it does not consist of transactions grouped into blocks that are stored in a chain, but as a stream of individual transactions entangled together. The main principle of the technology is that every user who intends to make a transaction has to validate two previous transactions on the Tangle, with the reward of his transaction being validated by another user (illustrated in **Figure 12**) (IOTA Foundation, 2018).

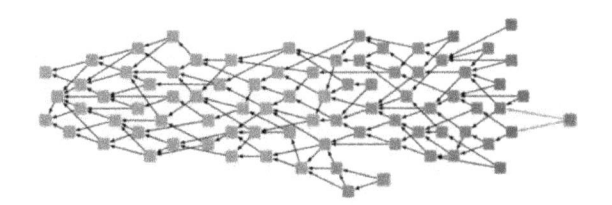

Figure 12: Transaction confirmation in the ITOA Tangle (IOTA Foundation, 2018)

Since every participant is a transaction validator, this eliminates the need for mining. As a result, IOTA transactions are completely feeless. This structure also enables high scalability of transactions. The more activity in the Tangle, the faster transactions can be confirmed. Moreover, without the need for monetary rewards, IOTA is not limited to payment settlements. It is possible to store information within Tangle enabling secure data transfers (IOTA Foundation, 2018).

IOTA was invented by David Sønstebø, Sergey Ivancheglo, Dominik Schiener, and Dr. Serguei Popov. Originally the group came together in 2014 to develop a brand-new type of ternary microprocessor for the internet of things (IoT) and distributed computing. At that point the team realized that there is a need for a secure and decentralized value and data settlement environment to enable the emergence of a machine economy.

Since all cofounders were deeply involved in DLT since 2010, they started to develop the IOTA protocol in early 2015 (HelloIOTA, n.d.). The crowdsale of the IOTA token took place in December 2015 with a total fund raise of about $500,000 worth of Bitcoin and other cryptocurrencies for the project development. It is important to note that there was no pre-allocation or special treatment to any of the founders or developers. Afterwards the founding team asked the crowdsale participants to donate a certain amount of issued IOTA tokens back with the aim of financing the IOTA Foundation. The foundation was established as a German non-profit organization ("gemeinnützige Stiftung") in November 2017 in Berlin with the objective of further developing the IOTA protocol and bringing together governments and industries to help achieve the IOTA vision (IOTA Foundation, 2018).

The token design may also have a major impact on the valuation of IOTA. The total supply of IOTA tokens is 2,779,530,283,277,761. This number is the result of $(3^{33}-1)/2$ which is the largest possible 33-digit ternary number and optimized for ternary computation. This high supply is ideal for enabling micro-transactions among machines. In general, the unit MIOTA is used (for example on crypto exchanges) representing one million IOTA tokens. All tokens were created in the so-called genesis transaction (term for the first transaction in the Tangle). This means that you cannot create new tokens by mining, as in the case of Bitcoin, and the total amount of tokens will always remain the same (IOTA Foundation, 2018).

Concerning the token class, it appears that the IOTA token is a hybrid token with features of a cryptocurrency and a utility token. It is supposed to serve as a medium of exchange, store of value and unit of account of the machine economy, specialized in micro payments among devises, which clearly makes it a cryptocurrency. On the other hand, it also offers concrete utilities to its holders. As already stated the IOTA Tangle can also be used as a medium for secure data transfers. The foundation already established a data marketplace with several leading companies where sensor data can be traded (Ponciano, 2017). Other use cases include, for example, digital citizen identification in Taipei, Taiwan or supply chain solutions. Also, the new IOTA project "qubic" that was released in June 2018, plans to provide further utility features such as smart contracts or outsourcing computer power (Golstein, 2018). Moreover, the IOTA Foundation recently launched the Ecosystem Development Fund that aims to incentivize developers to create more IOTA use cases (Lange, 2018). So, all in all, IOTA derives its value from serving as a cryptocurrency as well as from its increasing utility. The following section tries to quantify this fundamental value by using an earlier presented valuation model.

5.2 Valuation of IOTA

With a current total market cap of around $3 billion, IOTA ranks among the top 10 of the largest crypto assets worldwide, whereas many market observers are wondering whether there is any fundamental value justifying the IOTA price (CoinMarketCap, 2018). According to the cofounder Dominik Schiener it definitely does by stating that in future even a "one trillion-dollar market cap would be reasonable if IOTA becomes the backbone of IoT" (McIntosh, 2018). This section tries to determine the fundamental value of IOTA which should be by no mean a price target serving as an investment advice. It should rather help to identify the underlying value drivers within the IOTA crypto economy. The model is also useful to figure out what degree of adoption IOTA needs to achieve in order to justify certain price levels.

To carry out a valuation of the IOTA token the Equation of Exchange (proposed by Chris Burniske) was chosen since it represents the most sophisticated and suitable model for this purpose. The NVT ratio as well as the Metcalfe's Law are inappropriate because they are based on the daily transaction volume on the Tangle. Unfortunately, this number is currently not being measured. Secondly, even if the daily transaction volume was available, it can be assumed that the number would be highly distorted by transactions between wallets of the same user and spam transactions because remember, IOTA transactions are feeless. The cost of production approach is also not applicable to IOTA because as a non-mineable token, the IOTA token doesn't have any production costs.

The first step of applying the Equation of Exchange (MV = PQ) is to estimate the future total addressable market (TAM) of IOTA. IOTA's overall vision is to become the backbone of a machine economy by providing the distributed environment to settle feeless micropayments and data transfers between IoT devises. According to a market analysis conducted by GrowthEnabler & MarketsandMarkets the five dominating IoT sectors by market share are: 1. Smart cities (26%), 2. Industrial IoT (24%), 3. Connected health (20%), 4. Smart homes (14%) and 5. Connected cars (7%) (GrowthEnabler, 2017). For the analysis these five IoT sectors are used as IOTA's main target markets. However, IoT will probably not be the only use case of IOTA. Due to its feeless transactions it could also revolutionize the financial sector especially the way people pay each other. Therefore, two other application fields are added to the scope of future IOTA implementation: E-commerce and P2P payments. In the following, the seven main application areas of IOTA will be described in more detail by showing what efforts the IOTA Foundation and community undertook to push forward the IOTA adoption into these areas:

Smart cities

Smart cities are about digitalizing urban areas in order to manage resources more efficiently. This includes for example traffic management, water distribution, waste management, urban security and environmental monitoring. Smart cities are expected to generate the biggest share of the future IoT market (GrowthEnabler, 2017). The IOTA Foundation is already part of some smart city initiatives in order to implement the IOTA technology and token in a connected urban environment. In early 2018 the capital of Taiwan, Taipei partnered with IOTA to develop smart city solutions, starting with a digital citizen identification system based on IOTA's TangleID technology (Blonde 2.0, 2018). In July 2018 IOTA and the European smart city consortium +CityxChange received green light from the EU Commission, under the "Smart Cities and Communities" call of the EU research and innovation program Horizon 2020 (Pimenta, 2018).

Industrial IoT

Implementing DLT in connected manufacturing devices, generally described as industrial IoT (IIoT), is one of IOTA's main objectives. A series of large industry corporations and industrial research institutions have already shown interest in the IOTA project. At the world's biggest industry exhibition 'Hannover Messe' companies such as Fujitsu and DXC Technology showcased industrial solutions based on IOTA technology (Rödder, 2018). Another example is the Industrial IOTA Lab Aachen, founded by the RWTH Aachen University to explore the potential of IOTA for the industrial production (RWTH Achen, 2018).

Connected health

IOTA aims to enable greater data integrity within the health industry by securely transmitting and storing individual medical records on the IOTA Tangle. Also, health and medical devices could be connected to the IOTA network. Therefore, IOTA partnered with healthcare providers for DLT research in Norway such as the Norwegian Centre for E-Health Research and Oslo Cancer Cluster (Mandelli, 2017).

Smart homes

Since IOTA enables micropayments and data streams between all kind of connected devices it could serve as a platform to manage smart homes including devices such as thermostats, appliances, entertainment systems or security systems. For example, it might enable to purchase grocery items from an e-commerce site by using a connected fridge, paid in IOTA tokens. Or, a house owner could set up a solar panel and sell the surplus of solar power to his neighbor (IOTA Foundation, 2018).

Connected cars

Connected cars, or smart mobility in a wider sense, is a key area of the IOTA adoption. According to the IOTA Foundation cars will be able to pay autonomously for parking, charging, tolls or any other service. On the other hand, cars can earn money by, for example, delivering items or providing care sharing services. IOTA aims to be the standard for transactions and sharing data in this new transportation ecosystem (IOTA

Foundation, 2018). Therefore, they partnered with a range of big automotive companies such as Volkswagen and Bosch. On the latest CeBIT, the world largest trade fair for innovation and digitalization, Volkswagen presented a Proof of Concept (PoC) that uses the IOTA Tangle for "over-the-air" software updates in the car. The IOTA Foundation is also part of the Mobility Open Blockchain Initiative (MOBI) along with BMW, Renault, Ford, GM, Bosch and IBM (Suberg, 2018). IOTA also presented the world's first IOTA smart charging station, a PoC where electric cars can be charged by paying with IOTA tokens (IOTA Foundation, 2018).

E-commerce

IOTA is not explicitly designed to be used for e-commerce. However, there have been many efforts from the IOTA community to implement IOTA in e-commerce. For example, the community-driven project PayIOTA helps web merchants to accept IOTA payments easily on their websites with no fees (Payiota, 2018). The website www.iotashops.com is committed to list all online shops that are accepting IOTA as a payment.

P2P payments

Due to the feeless transactions, IOTA has also a strong potential of being implemented as a medium for P2P payments, especially for cross-border remittances which are currently characterized by very high fees and transaction delays. The recently released IOTA Trinity wallet was a huge step to facilitate P2P transactions as it enables very user-friendly and secure settlements of IOTA token payments.

It needs to be emphasized that the list of IOTA's application areas makes no claim to being complete and could certainly be extended. Other possible markets are for example data trading, smart contracts or outsourced computation. But these areas are often overlapping with the listed ones (e.g. data trading) or very hard to quantify (e.g. outsourced computation) because there is no market research yet.

Based on the selected target markets, the next step is to estimate the size of these markets that will form the future IOTA economy (represented by PQ in the Equation of

Exchange). This is done by conducting a top-down analysis of the future market based on forecasts of market research firms. Since an investment period of 10 years is assumed, the market volumes in the year 2028 are projected. The first column of **Table 4** shows the predicted market sizes of IOTA's target markets by 2028. The volumes for the IoT areas are based on the IoT forecast report conducted by the market research firm MarketsandMarkets and are derived from the revenues of IoT services. According to the report, the IoT market is expected to grow to $561.04 billion by the year 2022, at a Compound Annual Growth Rate (CAGR) of 26.9% (MarketsandMarkets, 2017). The CAGR of 26.9% is used to estimate the market volume until 2028. Keep in mind that very pessimistic IoT market predictions were chosen. There are other forecasts of market research companies such as McKinsey estimating the total potential economic impact of IoT to be $3.9 to $11.1 trillion per year in 2025 (McKinsey, 2015). The predictions for the future e-commerce and P2P payments markets are taken from the online statistics portal Statista (see **Appendix 1 and 2** for more details). In the second column of **Table 4** you see the percentage of the predicted market volume that is addressable to IOTA. Generally, it can be assumed that there will be countries restricting DLT, especially cryptocurrencies, which will make the market entry for IOTA more difficult. For the IoT areas it is estimated that around 75% is addressable to IOTA. For E-commerce and P2P payments, it can be assumed that smaller percentages will be addressable to IOTA because these two areas do not represent the main focus of IOTA and there are already well-established systems enabling efficient payment processes:

Target market	Predicted market volume 2028 (bn $)	Addressable for IOTA (%)	Addressable for IOTA (bn $)
Smart cities	609	75%	457
Industrial IoT	562	75%	422
Connected Health	469	75%	351
Smart homes	328	75%	246
Connected cars	164	75%	123
E-commerce	12,976	10%	1,298
P2P payments	309	30%	93
Total	**15.417**		**2,989**

Table 4: IOTA target markets in 2028 (GrowthEnabler, 2017; Statista 2018)

The analysis also requires a projection of the percent penetration that IOTA will take of total addressable market (TAM). To do so a S-curve is used that shows the degree of adoption of a new technology or product in three phases (Burniske, 2017):

- 0-10%: Introduction (slow growth)
- 10-90%: take over time (rapid growth)
- 10-100%: Saturation (slow growth)

The S curve is based on the following formula (Burniske, 2017):

$$\text{Market penetration} = \frac{Saturation\ percentage}{1+81^{\wedge}\left(start\ of\ fast\ growth + \frac{takeover\ time}{2} - base\ year\right)/takeover\ time}$$

with,

Saturation percentage = maximum share the crypto network will take of its TAM
Base year = when the crypto network will launch and adoption will start
Start of fast growth = year when 10% of its saturation percentage will be hit
Takeover time = Amount of years it takes to go from 10% to 90% of its saturation percentage

In this analysis 2019 is assumed to be the base year where the IOTA adoption will start. The year 2020 is defined as the start of fast growth and the takeover time is estimated to be 7 years. An estimated saturation percentage of 30% of the TAM by IOTA, results in the following S curve over the next 10 years (**Figure 13**):

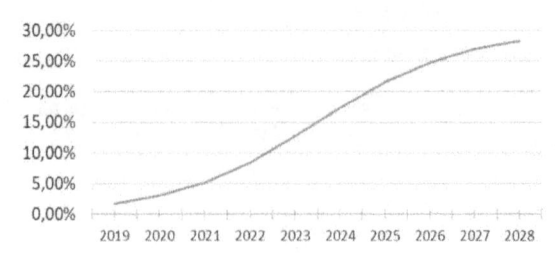

Figure 13: Percent penetration of IOTA from 2019 to 2028 (own illustration)

The Excel analysis in the appendices (**Appendix A**) comprises three different scenarios: a pessimistic scenario (10% of TAM), a base scenario (30% of TAM) and an optimistic scenario (50% of TAM). Keep in mind that IOTA's objective is to become a global industry standard which means that it would take at least 50% of the TAM. For the sake of simplicity, it is continued with the base scenario (30% of TAM). So, under the assumption of 30% saturation of the TAM, the IOTA economy (PQ) is expected to be around $846.6 billion by the year 2028.

At this point the velocity comes into the play, because remember the monetary base (projected market cap) is M = (PQ)/V. The velocity measures how many times an IOTA token changes hands in one year. Unfortunately, there is no data for the velocity of the IOTA token yet. That's why the velocity of Bitcoin and USD is used as a benchmark. Bitcoin's velocity in the year 2017 was around 5.66 (Janashia, 2018). The velocity of the USD M1 money stock is about 5.5 at the time of writing (FRED, 2018). Since IOTA is feeless and enables microtransactions one can expect a higher velocity than Bitcoin that is mainly used as a store of value. That's way the IOTA velocity is estimated to be around 10 in the year 2028 which is about two times Bitcoin's and USD velocity. Currently IOTA's velocity is probably much lower since most IOTA holders store their IOTA tokens for investment purposes which results in a low velocity.

Now, the Equation of Exchange M = (PQ)/V can be used to calculate the required monetary base of IOTA in the year 2028. Dividing the future IOTA GDP of $846.6 billion (PQ) by the velocity of 10 (V) results in a monetary base of $84.7 billion. This means that IOTA's total market cap will have to be worth $84.7 billion in order to serve the projected economy of $846.6 billion. The value per MIOTA would then be $30.46 in 2028.

Since this value represents the future utility value of IOTA another key concept of Chris Burniske's valuation model needs to be applied: Discount rates. Since an investment in IOTA is associated with very high risk, as all crypto assets, a discount rate of 30% seems to be reasonable. Similar discount rates a used to calculate the present value of investments in startups. So, discounting the future utility value of 2028 with a discount rate of 30% results in a present value of $2.21 per MIOTA. Comparing this value to the current market price of around $1.00 per MIOTA it can be concluded that the IOTA token is currently undervalued.

The optimistic scenario with 50% penetration of the TAM results in a future utility value of $50.77 per MIOTA in 2028 and a present value of $3.68 per MIOTA. This would also indicate a current undervaluation of IOTA. The pessimistic scenario (10% of TAM) reveals a future utility value of $10.15 per MIOTA and a present value of $0.74 per MIOTA. In the pessimistic scenario it could be stated that IOTA is currently overvalued. However, the results of the optimistic and the pessimistic scenario could be used as a lower and upper bound for the IOTA valuation. So, it could be summarized that the expected fundamental value of IOTA will reach $10 to $50 per MIOTA by the year 2028 which is a present value of $0.75 to $3.7 per MIOTA. In the last 6 months the price of the IOTA token moved more or less in these ranges. Only, in December 2017 bullish outbreaks above $5 per MIOTA could be observed.

Of course, these numbers have to be treated very cautiously. The calculated fundamental value of IOTA is mainly derived from the speculative future value rather than current utility value. However, this doesn't differ much from traditional valuation approaches where projected future returns are used in order to calculate the present value of stocks. Also note that IOTA, as nearly all crypto assets, are still Proof of Concept, meaning that mass adoption has not taken place yet and any investment in its token can be considered as a risky bet on weather the project will reach the adoption goals of its potentially groundbreaking technology or not. A major risk for IOTA is the very competitive DLT market. There are also other technologies designed for IoT (such as IoT Chain or WaltonChain) and it is hard to say who will be the winner in that race. By looking at the amount of high quality partnerships and the development time of over 5 years IOTA seems to be well ahead at the moment. Other risks are related to the financial capacity of the IOTA foundation, the technical feasibility, the regulatory environment, the community acceptance and the marketing strategy. All of these factors will have a great impact on the future of IOTA. However, this risk is very hard to quantify and further research on this is necessary.

Another crucial drawback of the IOTA valuation is the high sensitivity to the input parameters, such as the projected IOTA economy (PQ), the velocity (V) and the discount rate. In order to estimate PQ it was necessary to identify the target markets of IOTA as well as the future market volumes and IOTA market share. These numbers are very much based on personal assumptions or forecast reports of market research firms that can vary extremely. The velocity is also hard to predict as there is no data on IOTA's velocity yet. The velocity also depends on the willingness of IOTA holder to spend the token. Since the IOTA token has a fixed supply and there is no possibility to regulate inflation in the token design of IOTA it is highly questionable if IOTA holders will have an incentive to spend their tokens.

In general, it can be said that the output of the valuation is only as good as the assumptions made for the inputs. Since these assumptions are very subjective the results of the fundamental analysis should not serve as a price target or an investment advice. However, the model helps to figure out what happens to the value of the IOTA token if certain conditions are assumed. It also helps to determine what level of adoption IOTA needs achieve in order to reach certain price levels. This is why the Equation of Exchange can be considered as a very useful model to analyze the value drivers of IOTA.

6. Conclusion

Referring to the first research question of **how the fundamental value of crypto assets can be determined**, the thesis revealed that crypto assets can be evaluated as an investment, a currency, a network or as a product. Depending the nature und purpose of the crypto asset different models can be applied (second research question: **Which valuation techniques can be applied to the different token type?**). Traditional valuation techniques, such as the DCF and CAPM consider crypto assets as an investment vehicle comparable to stocks. The original form of the DCF can only be applied to tokens with fixed returns (security tokens, staking tokens…). However, an adjusted DCF formula where the future cash flow is replaced by future utility value could be applied to almost all current crypto assets. A crypto CAPM could be formulated when crypto assets become mature enough in order to define the required variables, such as the volatility indicator beta. The Equation of Exchange, which is the most popular and currently most useful model, looks at crypto assets as a currency serving a specific "mini economy". Theoretically it could be applied to all cryptocurrencies as well as utility tokens. Other valuation models, such as the NVT ratio and Metcalfe's Law treat crypto assets as networks that derive their value from the number of users or the transaction volume between those users. Hence, these valuation models are only applicable to network tokens that are tied to the development of a network, which is usually the case for cryptocurrencies and utility tokens, but not security and asset backed tokens. The cost of production approach values crypto assets as a commodity with production costs. Obviously, this model can only be applied to mineable tokens that are produced under energy consumption. Finally, the accessibility discount is rather a phenomenon describing an undervaluation of crypto assets due to limited accessibility then a comprehensive valuation technique. The idea can be applied to all tradable crypto assets.

Beside the limited applicability of most of the models, they have other major drawbacks. Some of them, such as the asset rotation theory or the concept of accessibility discount, are too simplistic in order to derive a fundament value. The Equation of Exchange suffers very much from its sensitivity to its input parameters, such as the velocity. The NVT ratio as well as Metcalfe's Law are calculated based on the on-chain transaction volume which is doubted to be the only value driver. They also tend to be an indicator for price movements rather that determining the fundamental value. The cost of production approach states that the fundamental value simply equals the production costs. However, the causality of production costs and value of a mineable token, such as Bitcoin is not definitely proven.

Due to these limitations, much research is yet to be done in the field of crypto asset valuation. As the crypto market matures more market data will be available that can be used to analyze the value drivers of crypto assets in order to improve current valuation frameworks. This will be very important to attract new investors and establish crypto assets as a new asset class. For today, it is important that investors take all applicable valuation techniques into consideration which could help to estimate the fundamental value in a range between lower and upper bounds of value. Furthermore, they should combine quantitative analysis, presented in this thesis, with qualitative research including factors, such as the quality of the team, whitepaper, underlying technology, community, token design and market timing.

In the second part of the thesis, the Equation of Exchange was applied to the IOTA token in order to answer the third research question: **What is the fundamental value of the IOTA token?** The analysis revealed that the fundamental value of IOTA could reach 10 to $50 per MIOTA by the year 2028. Using a discount rate of 30% this results in a present value of $0.75 to $3.7 per MIOTA. Compared to the current market price of around 1$ per MIOTA it can be said that IOTA is neither under- nor overvalued. The valuation is based on the assumption that IOTA will be widely adopted in the IoT market (smart cities, industrial IoT, connected health, smart homes and connected cars) as well as for e-commerce and P2P payments. However due to the risks of the IOTA project and the discussed limitations of the valuation model these numbers should be treated with caution. As time goes by and the IOTA adoption starts the model should be updated regularly.

List of references

Belvedere, M. J., 2018, '*Bitcoin bull Tom Lee wants Wall Street to know he didn't cut his year-end forecast*', CNBC, viewed 20 July 2018, <https://www.cnbc.com/2018/07/05/fundstrats-tom-lee-cuts-his-year-end-bitcoin-forecast-to-20000.html>.

Blonde 2.0, 2018, '*Taipei City to use IOTA's distributed ledger technology for smart city*', viewed 20 July 2018, <https://pr.blonde20.com/iota-taipei/>.

Bruniske, C., 2018, Twitter, viewed 20 July 2018, <https://twitter.com/cburniske/status/952625373614870534>.

Burniske, C., 2017, '*Cryptoasset Valuations*', Medium, viewed 20 July 2018, <https://medium.com/@cburniske/cryptoasset-valuations-ac83479ffca7>.

Burniske, C. & Tatar, J., 2018, '*Cryptoassets - The Innovative Investor's Guide to Bitcoin and Beyond*', 1st edition, McGraw Hill Education, New York.

BusinessDictionary, n.d., '*What is an asset? Definition and meaning*', viewed 20 July 2018, <http://www.businessdictionary.com/definition/asset.html>.

Cameron, A. & Trinh, K., 2017, '*Bitcoin: Four reasons driving the cryptocurrency's price jumps and bumps*', ABC News, viewed 20 July 2018, <http://www.abc.net.au/news/2017-11-14/bitcoin-price-what-is-behind-the-jumps-and-bumps/9145600>.

Cheng, E., 2018, '*Bill Gates: I would short bitcoin if I could*', CNBC, viewed 20 July 2018, <https://www.cnbc.com/2018/05/07/bill-gates-i-would-short-bitcoin-if-i-could.html>.

CoinMarketCap, 2018, viewed 20 July 2018, <https://coinmarketcap.com/all/views/all/>.

Coinmetrics, 2018a, '*On the difficulty of estimating on-chain transaction volume*', viewed 20 July 2018, <https://coinmetrics.io/difficulty-estimating-chain-transaction-volume/>.

Coinmetrics, 2018b, viewed 20 July 2018, <https://coinmetrics.io/>.

Cong, L. W., Li, Y. & Wang, N., 2018, '*Tokenomics: Dynamic Adoption and Valuation*', Research paper No. 18-46, Columbia Business School, New York, USA.

D'Onorio Demeo, L. & Young, C., 2017, '*Valuing Crypto Assets*', draft research paper, American Economic Association, Nashville, Tennessee, USA.

Digiconomist, 2018, viewed 20 July 2018, <https://digiconomist.net/bitcoin-energy-consumption>.

Evans, A., 2018, '*On Value, Velocity and Monetary Theory - A New Approach to Cryptoasset Valuations*', Medium, viewed 20 July 2018, <https://medium.com/blockchannel/on-value-velocity-and-monetary-theory-a-new-approach-to-cryptoasset-valuations-32c9b22e3b6f>.

EY, 2018, '*IFRS (#) - Accounting for crypto-assets*', viewed 20 July 2018, available at <https://www.ey.com/Publication/vwLUAssets/EY-IFRS-Accounting-for-crypto-assets/$File/EY-IFRS-Accounting-for-crypto-assets.pdf>.

FRED, 2018, '*Velocity of M1 Money Stock*', Federal Reserve Bank of St. Louis, viewed 20 July 2018, <https://fred.stlouisfed.org/series/M1V>.

Fung, B., 2018, '*Bitcoin and ether shouldn't be regulated like stocks and bonds, a top SEC official says*', Washington Post, viewed 20 July 2018, <https://www.washingtonpost.com/news/the-switch/wp/2018/06/14/bitcoin-and-ether-shouldnt-be-regulated-like-stocks-and-bonds-a-top-sec-official-says/?noredirect=on&utm_term=.0e0f912b34fd>.

Golstein, S., 2018, '*IOTA Releases Details of Major Project, Qubic*', Finance Magnets, viewed 20 July 2018, <https://www.financemagnates.com/cryptocurrency/news/iota-releases-details-major-project-qubic/>.

GrowthEnabler, 2017, '*Market Pulse Report, Internt of Things*', viewed 20 July 2018, < https://growthenabler.com/flipbook/pdf/IOT%20Report.pdf>.

Hahn, C. & Wons, A., 2018, '*Initial Coin Offering (ICO). Unternehmensfinanzierung auf Basis der Blockchain-Technologie*', Springer Gabler-Verlag, 1st edition, Wiesbaden, Germany.

Hayes, A., 2015, '*Cryptocurrency Value Formation: An Empirical Analysis Leading to a Cost of Production Model for Valuing Bitcoin*', Reearch Paper, The New School for Social Research, New York, USA.

Hayes, A., 2018, '*Bitcoin price and its marginal cost of production: support for a fundamental value*', Research Paper, University of Wisconsin-Madison, Department of Sociology, Wisconsin, USA.

HelloIOTA, n.d., '*What is IOTA?*', viewed 20 July 2018, <https://helloiota.com/what-is-iota/>.

Henry, P. E., Robinson, T. R. & Stowe, J. D., 2010, *'Equity Asset Valuation'*, 2nd edition, John Wiley & Sons, Hoboken, New Jersey.

Horsley, H., 2017, *'2017: The Year Crypto Became a New Asset Class'*, CoinDesk, viewed 20 July 2018, <https://www.coindesk.com/2017-year-crypto-became-new-asset-class/>.

Hosp, J., 2017, *'Cryptocurrencies - Bitcoin, Ethereum, Blockchain, ICO's & Co. simply explained'*, Julian Hosp Coaching LTD, 1st edition.

Huillet, M., 2019, *'Coinbase Custody' Targeting Institutional Investors Now 'Officially Open for Business'*, Cointelegraph, viewed 20 July 2018, <https://cointelegraph.com/news/coinbase-custody-targeting-institutional-investors-now-officially-open-for-business>.

IOTA Foundation, 2018, viewed 20 July 2018, <https://www.iota.org/>.

Janashia, N., 2018, *'Bitcoin - 2017 Velocity Analysis'*, Medium, viewed 20 July 2018, <https://medium.com/@Nodar/bitcoin-2017-velocity-analysis-5d91b8906bb3>.

Kalichkin, D., 2018a, *'Rethinking Network Value to Transactions (NVT) Ratio'*, Medium, viewed 20 July 2018, <https://medium.com/cryptolab/https-medium-com-kalichkin-rethinking-nvt-ratio-2cf810df0ab0>.

Kalichkin, D., 2018b, *'Rethinking Metcalfe's Law applications to cryptoasset valuation'*, Medium, viewed 20 July 2018, <https://medium.com/cryptolab/network-value-to-metcalfe-nvm-ratio-fd59ca3add76>.

Kalla, S., 2017, *'A Framework for Valuing Crypto Tokens'*, CoinDesk, viewed 20 July 2018, <https://www.coindesk.com/framework-valuing-crypto-tokens/>.

Kasch, M. & Sarkar, A., 2011, *'Is There an S&P 500 Index Effect?'*, Staff Report No. 484, Federal Reserve Bank, New York, USA.

Koenig, A., 2017, *'Cryptocoins. Investieren in digitale Währungen'*, FinanzBuch Verlag, Munich, Germany.

Lange, G., 2018, *'IOTA Ecosystem ist live'*, Kryptoszene, viewed 20 July 2018, <https://kryptoszene.de/iota-ecosystem-ist-live/>.

Lannquist, A., 2018, *'Today's Crypto Asset Valuation Frameworks'*, viewed 20 July 2018, <https://blockchainatberkeley.blog/todays-crypto-asset-valuation-frameworks-573a38eda27e>.

Mandelli, A., 2017, *'IOTA Partners Healthcare Providers for Blockchain Research in Norway'*, CCN, viewed 20 July 2018, <https://www.ccn.com/iota-spearheads-dlt-research-in-norway/>.

MarketsandMarkets, 2017, *'Internet of Things (IoT) market - Global forecast to 2022'*, market research report, report code: TC 2895, available at <https://www.marketsandmarkets.com/Market-Reports/internet-of-things-market-573.html>.

McIntosh, R., 2018, *'IOTA Co-Founder: the Coin Will "Definitely Be Among Top 3 Cryptos in 2018'*, Finance Magnets, viewed 20 July 2018, <https://www.financemagnates.com/cryptocurrency/interview/iota-co-founder-coin-will-definitely-among-top-3-cryptos-2018/>.

McKeon, S., 2017, *'Cryptoasset valuation - Approaches and challenges'*, viewed 20 July 2018, <https://www.slideshare.net/loukerner/crypto-valuation-prof-stephen-mckeon>.

McKinsey, 2015, *'The Internet of Things: Mapping the value beyond the hype'*, McKinsey Global Institute, available at <https://www.mckinsey.com/~/media/McKinsey/Business%20Functions/McKinsey%20Digital/Our%20Insights/The%20Internet%20of%20Things%20The%20value%20of%20digitizing%20the%20physical%20world/The-Internet-of-things-Mapping-the-value-beyond-the-hype.ashx>.

Nambiampurath, R., 2018, *'Bitcoin at $1 Million by 2020: McAfee Doubles Down on Bullish Bet'*, CCN, viewed 20 July 2018, <https://www.ccn.com/despite-bitcoin-crash-mcafee-holds-his-1-million-by-2020-bet/>.

Njui, J. P., 2018, *'Crypto Markets to Reach $20 Trillion Value,' says Billionaire Investor Mike Novogratz'*, EthereumWorldNews, viewed 20 July 2018, <https://ethereumworldnews.com/crypto-markets-to-reach-20-trillion-value-says-billionaire-investor-mike-novogratz/>.

Oliver, J., 2018, *'Cryptocurrencies: Last Week Tonight with John Oliver (HBO)'*, YouTube, viewed 20 July 2018, <https://www.youtube.com/watch?v=g6iDZspbRMg>.

Paul, A., 2017, *'How To Value Cryptocurrency Conference Call'*, Youtube, viewed 20 July 2018, <https://www.youtube.com/watch?v=Ira34zZJkuk>.

Payiota, 2018, viewed 20 July 2018, <https://payiota.me/>.

Ponciano, J., 2017, '*IOTA Foundation Launches Data Marketplace For 'Internet-Of-Things' Industry*', Forbes, viewed 20 July 2018, <https://www.forbes.com/sites/jonathanponciano/2017/11/28/iota-foundation-launches-data-marketplace-for-internet-of-things-research/#36fbc5b2f52b>.

Pimenta W., 2018, '*Green light from the EU Commission for IOTA and the European smart city consortium +CityxChange*', IOTA Foundation, viewed 20 July 2018, <https://blog.iota.org/green-light-from-the-eu-commission-for-iota-and-the-european-smart-city-consortium-cityxchange-f7928aef33ac>.

Rödder, V., 2018, '*Hannover Messe: Mehrere Unternehmen stellen Use Cases mit IOTA vor*', Base58, viewed 20 July 2018, <https://base58.de/iota-auf-der-hannovermesse-vertreten/>.

RWTH Achen, 2018, '*IOTA for real-life industrial applications*', viewed 20 July 2018, <https://www.wzl.rwth-aachen.de/cms/www_content/en/dc5f626f19bbf8f1c125826700371c46/pressrelease_iota.en.pdf>.

Samani, K., 2017a, '*Bitcoin Is Better Than Digital Gold*', viewed 20 July 2018, <https://multicoin.capital/2017/09/21/bitcoin-better-digital-gold/>.

Samani, K., 2017b, '*The Blockchain Token Velocity Problem*', CoinDesk, viewed 20 July 2018, <https://www.coindesk.com/blockchain-token-velocity-problem/>.

Sams, R., 2014, 'T*he Marginal Cost of Cryptocurrency*', viewed 20 July 2018, <https://cryptonomics.org/2014/01/15/the-marginal-cost-of-cryptocurrency/>.

Shen, M., 2018, '*The EU's Biggest ETF Firm Expands Into Crypto Products*', CoinDesk, viewed 20 July 2018, <https://www.coindesk.com/the-eus-biggest-etf-firm-expands-into-crypto-products/>.

Silverstein, S., 2017, '*Analyst says 94% of bitcoin's price movement over the past 4 years can be explained by one equation*', Business Insider, viewed 20 July 2018, <https://www.businessinsider.de/bitcoin-price-movement-explained-by-one-equation-fundstrat-tom-lee-metcalf-law-network-effect-2017-10?r=US&IR=T>.

Suberg, W., 2018, '*Coinbase Retracts Announcement of Regulatory Approval to List Coins Considered Securities*', Cointelegraph, viewed 20 July 2018,

<https://cointelegraph.com/news/coinbase-retracts-announcement-of-regulatory-approval-to-list-coins-considered-securities>.

Urban, R., 2017, '*Bitcoin Is the New Crisis Currency*', Bloomberg, viewed 20 July 2018, <https://www.bloomberg.com/news/articles/2017-11-17/bitcoin-emerges-as-crisis-currency-in-hotspots-such-as-zimbabwe>.

Weber, W., 2018, '*The Quantity Theory of Money for Tokens*', Medium, viewed 20 July 2018, <https://blog.coinfund.io/the-quantity-theory-of-money-for-tokens-dbfbc5472423>.

Wikipedia, n.d., '*Definition of intrinsic value*', viewed 20 July 2018, <https://en.wikipedia.org/wiki/Intrinsic_value_(finance)#cite_note-1>.

Wikipedia, n.d., '*Definition of asset classes*', viewed 20 July 2018, <https://en.wikipedia.org/wiki/Asset_classes>.

Woo, W., 2017, '*Is Bitcoin In A Bubble? Check The NVT Ratio*', Forbes, viewed 20 July 2018, <https://www.forbes.com/sites/wwoo/2017/09/29/is-bitcoin-in-a-bubble-check-the-nvt-ratio/#20a1eaeb6a23>.

Woo, W., 2018, '*Bitcoin NVT Ratio*', viewed 20 July 2018, <http://charts.woobull.com/bitcoin-nvt-ratio/>.

World Bank, 2017, '*Distributed Ledger Technology (DLT) and Blockchain*', FinTech Note No. 1, Washington DC, USA.

World Gold Council, n.d., viewed 20 July 2018, <https://www.gold.org/>.

Zhang, X.-Z., Liu, J.-J. & Xu, Z.-W., 2015. *Tencent and Facebook Data Validate Metcalfe's Law,* Journal of computer science and technology, No. 30(2): 246–251.

Appendices

Appendix 1: Excel analysis of the IOTA valuation (based on Equation of Exchange)

	2019	2020	2021	2022	2023	2024	2025	2026	2027	2028
Total IOTA in calculation (MIOTA)	2.779.530.283,28	2.779.530.283,28	2.779.530.283,28	2.779.530.283,28	2.779.530.283,28	2.779.530.283,28	2.779.530.283,28	2.779.530.283,28	2.779.530.283,28	2.779.530.283,28

	2019	2020	2021	2022	2023	2024	2025	2026	2027	2028
Smart cities	71	91	115	146	185	235	298	378	480	609
Industrial IoT	68	94	166	185	171	217	275	349	443	562
Connected health	55	70	88	112	142	181	229	291	369	469
Smart homes	38	49	62	79	100	126	161	204	258	328
Connected cars	19	24	31	39	50	63	80	102	129	164
E-commerce	3456	4135	4878	5610	6451	7419	8532	9811	11283	12976
P2P Payments	80	100	125	156	195	177	203	234	269	309
Total	**3786**	**4553**	**5399**	**6254**	**7253**	**8418**	**9778**	**11369**	**13232**	**15417**

Smart cities	75%				
Industrial IoT	15%				
Connected health	75%				
Smart homes	75%				
Connected cars	10%				
E-commerce	10%				
P2P Payments	10%				

	2019	2020	2021	2022	2023	2024	2025	2026	2027	2028
Smart cities	54	68	86	109	139	176	224	284	360	457
Industrial IoT	49	63	80	101	128	163	206	262	332	422
Connected health	41	52	66	84	107	136	172	218	277	351
Smart homes	29	37	46	59	75	95	120	153	194	246
Connected cars	14	18	23	29	37	47	60	76	97	123
E-commerce	345	414	488	561	645	742	853	981	1128	1298
P2P Payments	25	30	36	40	46	53	63	70	81	93
Total addressable market (TAM)	**558**	**682**	**825**	**984**	**1177**	**1412**	**1697**	**2044**	**2469**	**2989**

(own creation)

Adoption Curve Inputs

Base Year	2019
Saturation Percentage Conservative	0
Saturation Percentage Base	0
Saturation Percentage Optimistic	0
Start of Fast Growth	
Take Over Time	

Scenarios

Conservative scenario	0
Base scenario	1
Optimistic scenario	0
Saturation used for calculation	30%

Adoption Curve Output

	2019	2020	2021	2022	2023	2024	2025	2026	2027	2028
Percent Penetration of the TAM	1,68%	3,00%	5,17%	8,42%	12,66%	17,34%	21,58%	24,83%	27,00%	28,32%

Percent Penetration of IOTA Each Year

(Chart: percentages from 0% to 30% across years 2019–2028)

Capacity Supported by IOTA

	2019	2020	2021	2022	2023	2024	2025	2026	2027	2028
Total (=PQ)	9,4	20,5	42,6	82,8	149,1	244,7	366,2	507,6	666,7	846,6

IOTA as a Monetary Base Required (=S FU)

	2019	2020	2021	2022	2023	2024	2025	2026	2027	2028
	9,4	10,2	14,2	20,7	29,8	40,8	52,3	63,5	74,1	84,7

Valuation

	2019	2020	2021	2022	2023	2024	2025	2026	2027	2028
Utility Value per Miota	3,37	3,68	5,11	7,45	10,73	14,67	18,82	22,83	26,65	30,46
Discount rate										
Present value of Miota (based on end of investment)	2,59	2,18	2,33	2,61	2,85	3,04	3,00	2,80	2,51	2,21

(own creation)

Appendix 2: E-commerce sales worldwide 2014 to 2021 in billion USD

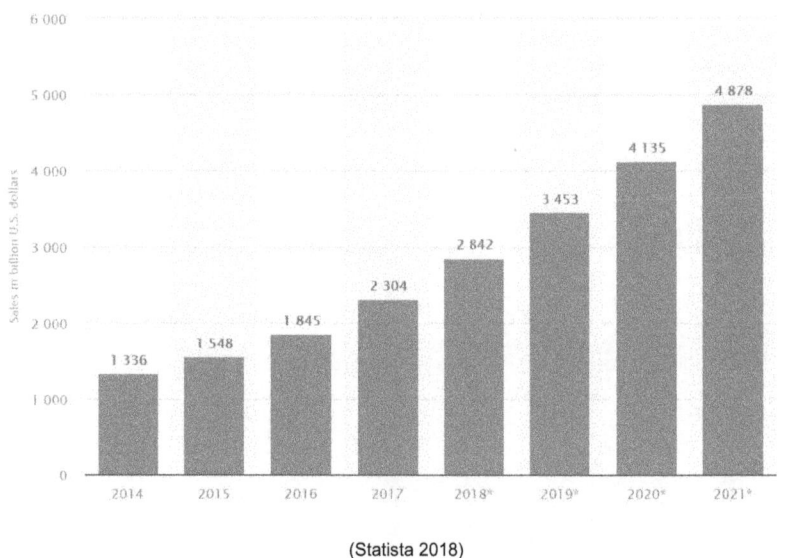

Year	Sales (billion USD)
2014	1 336
2015	1 548
2016	1 845
2017	2 304
2018*	2 842
2019*	3 453
2020*	4 135
2021*	4 878

(Statista 2018)

Description: "This statistic gives information on retail e-commerce sales worldwide from 2014 to 2021. In 2017, retail e-commerce sales worldwide amounted to 2.3 trillion US dollars and e-retail revenues are projected to grow to 4.88 trillion US dollars in 2021. The top 3 online stores' revenue amounted to almost 100 billion US dollars in 2017. Online shopping is one of the most popular online activities worldwide but the usage varies by region - in 2016, an estimated 19 percent of all retail sales in China occurred via internet but in Japan the share was only 6.7 percent. Desktop PCs are still the most popular device for placing online shopping orders but mobile devices, especially smartphones, are catching up" (Statista 2018).

Appendix 3: P2P Money Transfers worldwide 20146 to 2022 in billion USD

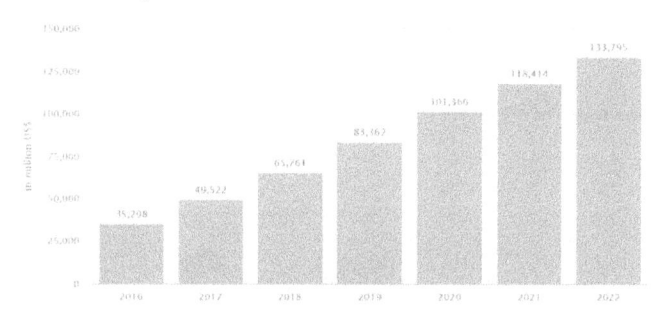

(Statista 2018)

Description: "Online Peer-to-Peer (P2P) Money Transfers are defined as money transfers made over the internet between private individuals. Cross-border payments and remittances are the most relevant segments for the FinTech market. Classic providers in this segment are credit institutions (banks), post offices and specialized money transfer services such as Western Union and Moneygram. Whereas traditional models of cross-border monetary transfer such as currency exchange, stationary stores and inter-bank transfers result in comparatively high time and monetary expense for users , "online-pure players" such as Transferwise, WorldRemit and Currency Cloud optimize the use of digital infrastructures to achieve time and cost savings." (Statista 2018)

In-scope:

- Online cross-border payments and remittance sending
- Money transfers processed by online-pure players (e.g. TransferWise)
- Transaction value equals money transfers out of the selected region

Out-of-scope:

- Social payments - payments via social networks
- Domestic Peer-to-Peer payments and bill splitting services
- Cross-border payments via traditional service providers (banks, post offices & Western Union, MoneyGram)

YOUR KNOWLEDGE HAS VALUE

- We will publish your bachelor's and master's thesis, essays and papers

- Your own eBook and book - sold worldwide in all relevant shops

- Earn money with each sale

Upload your text at www.GRIN.com and publish for free